TECHNICAL REPORT

Design of the Qatar National Research Fund

An Overview of the Study Approach and Key Recommendations

Victoria A. Greenfield, Debra Knopman, Eric Talley,
Gabrielle Bloom, Edward Balkovich, D. J. Peterson,
James T. Bartis, Stephen Rattien, Richard Rettig,
Mark Y. D. Wang, Michael Mattock, Jihane Najjar,
Martin C. Libicki

Prepared for the Qatar Foundation for Education, Science and
Community Development

RAND RAND-QATAR POLICY INSTITUTE

This research was sponsored by the Qatar Foundation for Education, Science, and Community Development and was conducted within the RAND-Qatar Policy Institute, a partnership of the RAND Corporation and the Qatar Foundation for Education, Science, and Community Development.

Library of Congress Cataloging-in-Publication Data

Design of the Qatar National Research Fund : an overview of the study approach and key recommendations / Victoria A. Greenfield ... [et al.].
    p. cm.
    Includes bibliographical references.
    ISBN 978-0-8330-4215-6 (pbk. : alk. paper)
    1. Qatar National Research Fund—Management. 2. Research—Qatar—Finance. 3. Intellectual property—Qatar. I. Greenfield, Victoria A., 1964–

Q180.Q2D47 2007
338.95363'06—dc22
                                                                                    2007036847

The RAND Corporation is a nonprofit research organization providing objective analysis and effective solutions that address the challenges facing the public and private sectors around the world. RAND's publications do not necessarily reflect the opinions of its research clients and sponsors.

RAND® is a registered trademark.

Published 2007 by the RAND Corporation
1776 Main Street, P.O. Box 2138, Santa Monica, CA 90407-2138
1200 South Hayes Street, Arlington, VA 22202-5050
4570 Fifth Avenue, Suite 600, Pittsburgh, PA 15213-2665
RAND URL: http://www.rand.org/
To order RAND documents or to obtain additional information, contact
Distribution Services: Telephone: (310) 451-7002;
Fax: (310) 451-6915; Email: order@rand.org

Preface

In 2004, the Qatar Foundation for Education, Science and Community Development asked the RAND-Qatar Policy Institute (RQPI) to recommend a design for the Qatar National Research Fund (QNRF) and then draft supporting business and implementation plans. The business plan presented the rationale and goals for QNRF, described the research environment in Qatar and the challenges it poses, proposed funding activities and an estimated minimum budget to support those activities, and outlined options for financing QNRF. The implementation plan provided details about how to launch, operate, and expand QNRF in the future.

In 2007, the Qatar Foundation formerly launched QNRF, based on the RQPI design. The purpose of this technical report is to archive publicly the core recommendations that the RQPI project team made in June 2004 to the Qatar Foundation for the design of QNRF. Therefore, the report itself is written in the future tense. Because the business and implementation plans are proprietary, they are not available for public distribution. Note also that this report is not intended to serve as a substitute for promotional material that may be developed to introduce QNRF to potential funders and recipients.

This report presents an overview of proposed business and implementation plans for QNRF along with supporting documentation. Appendixes include a comparative analysis of research-funding organizations and an analysis of models for managing intellectual property rights (IPRs). As implementation has proceeded, QNRF has adapted to changing circumstances and necessarily departed from the original RQPI organizational-design recommendations in some minor respects. Nonetheless, the authors hope that this material will be useful to policy leaders in other nations, particularly the Middle East, seeking to establish a national research fund; analysts and consultants who may be asked to tackle a similar task; researchers seeking funding from QNRF; and others interested in the implementation of science policy, particularly in the Middle East. More detailed information about QNRF can be found at its Web site at http://www.qnrf.org/.

The RAND-Qatar Policy Institute

The work reported here was carried out by RAND Infrastructure, Safety, and Environment, a division of the RAND Corporation, and was funded by the Qatar Foundation. For more information about this report, contact Debra Knopman, vice president and director, RAND Infrastructure, Safety, and Environment. She can be reached by email at Debra_Knopman@ rand.org; by telephone at +1-703-413-1100, extension 5667; or by mail at RAND Corporation, 1200 South Hayes Street, Arlington, Virginia 22202-5050, USA.

RQPI is a partnership of the RAND Corporation and the Qatar Foundation. The aim of RQPI is to offer the RAND style of rigorous and objective analysis to clients in the greater Middle East. In serving clients in the Middle East, RQPI draws on the full professional resources of the RAND Corporation. For further information on RQPI, contact the director, Richard Darilek. He can be reached by email at Richard_Darilek@rand.org; by telephone at +974-492-7400; or by mail at P.O. Box 23644, Doha, Qatar.

Contents

Figures

Tables

Summary

Qatar is a nation with ambitious aspirations of stimulating local and regional development while taking a prominent place on the world stage as a leader in research and scholarship. As a critical first step toward realizing these ambitions, Qatar has resolved to establish a national funding vehicle to support research. The Qatar National Research Fund (QNRF) is the leading institution in Qatar dedicated to funding research in the national interest. It addresses priority economic and social needs and pursues opportunities to attract internationally recognized researchers to study topics of regional and global importance.

QNRF is a project of the Qatar Foundation for Education, Science, and Community Development, a nonprofit organization dedicated to cultivating the full potential of the Qatari people through a network of progressive research and educational centers. To lay the groundwork for the fund, the Qatar Foundation asked the RAND-Qatar Policy Institute (RQPI) to recommend a design for QNRF and draft accompanying business and implementation plans.

The RQPI team presented a design that took the best practices of internationally recognized research and academic institutions and tailored them to both the Qatar Foundation's vision for the fund and the nation's unique needs, challenges, and opportunities. Three strategic goals form the backbone of the design. These goals build on each other, with each taking increasing prominence as QNRF becomes established over time.

The design included a structure for QNRF and laid out the tasks necessary to build the fund, to be undertaken during three stages of implementation. A start-up phase would be followed by the launch of operations and programs, which would be followed, in turn, by initiatives to deepen and broaden the research agenda. The design also proposed a set of operating principles that would enable the fund to meet its strategic goals and perform in accordance with internationally recognized standards for awarding grants and overseeing grantees' performance.

Qatar's Vision of Becoming an International Research Center

Qatar recognizes the vital role that research and development play in giving a country a competitive edge in the global arena. It views excellence in scholarship, innovation, and creativity as a means of distinguishing itself among nations—economically, strategically, and socially.

But Qatar's vision of international prominence starts at home. At the heart of its aspirations is the desire to see world-class research taking place in Qatari facilities, with service to the national interest as the primary goal. In its view, research brings multiple national benefits. It will build the country's intellectual resources. It will expand and diversify the national economy. It will enhance the education of Qatar's citizens and the training of its workforce. And it will foster improvements in the health, well being, environment, and security of Qatar's people and those of the region.

When attractive opportunities are available to conduct research of this caliber in Qatar, the belief is that an international reputation will soon follow. Research done in Qatar will achieve increasing visibility around the world. Qatar will build a name as a unique venue for particular research areas. Internationally recognized researchers will be drawn to the country to initiate or join projects.

Currently, no other institution fills this role. QNRF's mission is to advance knowledge and education by supporting original, competitively selected research in the physical, life, and social sciences; engineering and technology; the arts; and the humanities. It will also fund workshops, conferences, partnerships, and a national research survey. From students to professionals, researchers working in the academic, private, and public sectors will be eligible for funding opportunities.

RAND-Qatar Policy Institute's Approach to Developing a Design for the Qatar National Research Fund

To develop the QNRF design and business and implementation plans, the RQPI team first worked with the Qatar Foundation to articulate the vision, mission, goals, and operating principles for the fund. The team proposed refinements to these elements as the study progressed. RQPI also launched a comparative analysis of established research funding organizations and intellectual property right (IPR) regimes that could serve as possible models for QNRF. However, it recognized the need to design an organization that would work well in Qatar's unique circumstances.

Qatari Research Environment

To learn about the research environment, the RQPI team consulted numerous individuals in Qatar and abroad. These consultants came from academia, the business world, government, and nongovernmental organizations. They provided their views on the current status of research in the country, the nation's research needs, opportunities to be pursued, and the likely constraints and challenges.

Model Institutions

The RQPI team compared internationally recognized public and private institutions and foundations in the United States, Canada, Europe, New Zealand, and the Arabian Gulf[1] region. Each is dedicated to the support of research. Most share one or more commonalities with the proposed QNRF—mission and goals, size, age, or financing mechanisms.

Points of comparison included organizational structure, principles of governance, award processes, funding mechanisms, monitoring and evaluation processes, and approaches to planning and growth. By gaining deeper insight into the various operational methods of successful institutions, the RQPI team could develop recommendations based on the best of proven approaches.

---

[1] *Arabian Gulf* is the name used here for the body of water that some readers may call the *Persian Gulf.*

Models for Intellectual Property Rights

The RQPI team did a second comparative analysis to provide a set of candidate models for managing QNRF's IPRs. The study focused on the key trade-offs involved in various IPR regimes. The team then examined those trade-offs through the lens of policy concerns relevant to Qatar and proposed potentially suitable models.

Qatar National Research Fund Work Will Meet National Needs While Building an International Profile

Research focused on meeting Qatar's national needs will be QNRF's top funding priority. The RQPI team's discussions with Qatari leaders and members of the Qatar Foundation board revealed several of the country's most pressing concerns:

- Improving the quality of education in Qatar to give citizens the high-level skills required to compete in the 21st-century economy
- Diversifying the Qatari economy to lessen its dependence on the energy sector
- Drawing more women into the Qatari workforce
- Improving water management.

Qatar also offers numerous research opportunities—lines of inquiry to which the country is particularly well suited. Many of these are in line with national needs. They include studies of marine biology in highly saline waters; social transformation, particularly the changing role of women; and genomics. Research opportunities would attract researchers from abroad and raise Qatar's profile beyond its borders.

Qatar National Research Fund Strategy: Pursue Overlapping Research Goals Over Time

The RQPI team looked at QNRF's vision and mission, the research environment in Qatar, the nation's most pressing needs, and its most promising opportunities. On this basis, it proposed three overarching strategic goals for QNRF. These goals also demarcate three strategic phases of development for the fund.

During the first strategic phase, QNRF will focus primarily on *building human capital*. Funding and activities will be aimed at

- educating and training Qatar-based graduates and medical students in world-class, basic and applied research methods
- enabling researchers to undertake multiyear projects and produce high-quality research results relevant to Qatar's needs and interests
- increasing collaboration among researchers based in Qatar
- facilitating contacts and collaborations between Qatari researchers and the international research community.

This initial phase will be followed by a second in which QNRF will concentrate on *meeting other national needs* while continuing to build human capital. Programs are designed to

- enable more Qatari men and women to assume leadership positions in Qatar's businesses, universities, and research institutes
- increase the participation of Qatari women in the workforce
- diversify Qatar's economy and improve its performance
- improve the quality of the environment and management of natural resources
- enhance the health and life spans of Qataris.

In a third, current strategic phase, QNRF will maintain its commitment to the first two goals but turn its attention primarily to *raising Qatar's international profile*. Efforts will be devoted to building the country's regional and international reputation for excellence in several research areas and encouraging private-sector sources to assume an increasing share of research funding.

Qatar National Research Fund Operations: Complete Key Tasks in Three Stages of Implementation

The timing of QNRF operations derives from the three strategic phases. The QNRF design specifies three stages of implementation: start-up, launch operations and programs, and deepen and broaden the research agenda. The Qatar Foundation will perform the majority of the designated operational tasks in the earliest stage. Once the QNRF staff is in place, it will assume a greater responsibility.

Start-Up
During the start-up stage, the Qatar Foundation will establish the business, legal, and financial basis for QNRF. It will also appoint the fund's staff and other key stakeholders. Key decisions to be made include a choice of operating principles, financial structure, and a policy on IPRs.

Organizational Structure. The RQPI team proposed the basic, board-led governance model similar to that of the National Science Foundation in the United States. A governing board of six members will establish the fund's overall direction, set policy, and provide oversight. A director will run the daily operations and report to the board. Other stakeholders include QNRF staff and members of an advisory council comprised of Qatari academic and business leaders.

Operating Principles. QNRF's operating principles will be established during the start-up stage. For example, *QNRF should provide service to Qatar. QNRF-funded research should have the potential to produce identifiable national benefits. Research grants must be based on merit. QNRF should actively publish and promote research results and activities.* These and other operating principles reflect the values of the Qatar Foundation. They will enable QNRF to achieve its goals and meet the challenges of the research environment in Qatar.

Financing. An endowment scheme—in which charitable donations over the years supplement a large initial grant—offers significant advantages for establishing QNRF's long-term orientation. In contrast, a mechanism to accept pay-as-you-go funding from an annual government appropriation has near-term advantages. Consequently, the RQPI team recommended that both approaches be adopted.

Intellectual Property Rights. The RQPI team concluded that either the prevailing international model or the Canadian model would strike an acceptable balance for QNRF. In the former, grantees would retain intellectual property and licensing rights, and QNRF would have to demonstrate the basis for any decision to claim an exception. In the latter, QNRF would formally retain the rights but would adopt a stated policy that assigns rights to grantees in most cases. Should QNRF declare an exception, the grantee would bear the onus of demonstrating that its decision was arbitrary.

The prevailing international model is advantageous in that grantees around the world are likely to know and understand it better than the Canadian model, whereas the Canadian model would make it much easier for QNRF to exercise its rights when clearly in the national interest.

Launch Operations and Programs

During this second stage, the primary goal will be to set research priorities and get programs up and running. QNRF cannot implement all of its planned programs at full funding in the first year; some ramp-up time will be required.

The National Priorities Research Program and the Undergraduate Research Experience Program are the first priorities. The National Priorities Research Program will be QNRF's largest funding activity, supporting multiyear projects of multiple investigators. Awards will go to studies that pertain to national needs or aspirations or that are related to some unique attribute of the country that will bring world-class researchers to Qatar. It will be the primary means by which QNRF addresses the nation's most pressing concerns and pursues research opportunities for which Qatar may have a comparative advantage.

The Undergraduate Research Experience Program will stimulate undergraduate research opportunities in Education City and Qatar University through individual and group projects led by faculty and other researchers.

Several other programs will follow these two programs:

- **Workshops, conferences, and short courses** in Qatar will bring domestic and international participants together, helping to connect researchers in Qatar with their colleagues abroad.
- **Joint ventures in innovative enterprises** will support applied research in a particularly promising area, with a goal of commercialization. Each project requires at least one Qatari partner.
- **Distinguished fellowships** will support internationally known researchers and individuals to reside in Qatar for several months to a year, so that they may share their expertise and talent with the Qatar community.
- The **Biennial National Research Survey** will summarize, every other year, all research conducted in Qatar.

Award processes will be established and implemented as soon as the initial programs begin operating. These include procedures for soliciting proposals, choosing among funding mechanisms, reviewing proposals, and awarding grants.

The RQPI design advises QNRF to take a two-pronged approach to developing requests for proposals: first by consulting with experts in a given field, and second by drawing from its own staff and advisors, whose priority is QNRF's mission and goals. It recommends keeping a list of funding mechanisms that provide flexible tools for supporting different types of projects. And the design strongly advocates a peer-review process for selections and awards, as this would be essential to establishing QNRF's institutional credibility within the international research community.

Another critical task during this second stage will be to implement monitoring and evaluation processes for both institutional- and project-level performance. Measures will be needed to cover not only impacts but planning and operations. For example, regular assessment of how QNRF is distributing funding across its portfolio is a key part of institutional monitoring. At the institutional level, evaluation should always strive to determine how well the fund is meeting its goals and advancing its mission. Formally incorporating outside views is vital to ensuring quality and transparency.

At the project and program levels, effectiveness is the fundamental measure. Indicators may include publications, reports, and patents, as well as how funds are used. While different types of programs—a research versus a workshop grant, for instance—may demand that QNRF tailor reporting requirements, certain basic requirements should apply uniformly. Annual and final progress reports would fall into this category.

Deepen and Broaden the Research Agenda

As QNRF builds its expertise and organizational capabilities, it can begin to consider expanding its program slate and initiating new priority research areas. Before embarking on this stage—approximately three to five years into the fund's lifespan—QNRF management should conduct a rigorous review of its programs and operations. Concurrently, it should approach key stakeholders for their views on the fund's long-term growth strategy. The information gathered will suggest when and how QNRF should expand. Success will depend on a clear plan of action that demonstrates how the proposed strategy will meet QNRF's needs and achieve its goals.

Overcoming Challenges Will Be a Long-Term Process

QNRF will face a number of challenges related to Qatar's current research environment, such as the following:

- The initial cohort of local students who might take part in research will come from undergraduate degree programs. This will make it harder to create and sustain competitive research programs in science and engineering.
- University faculty and private-sector research staff turn over at a fairly high rate. This will make it challenging to maintain long-term research programs and ensure that grantees are consistently aware of Qatar's national and private-sector needs.
- Qatar is currently isolated from the world's research centers. This separation will need to be reduced for Qatar's visibility to increase and for cross-border collaboration to become more frequent.

- Both within the Qatari public and private sectors and among Qataris in general, awareness of the benefits of research is low. People will need to better understand and value the contributions research can make to Qatar.

The Qatar Foundation has already begun to address some of these constraints by investing in Education City—a community of educational institutions with campuses in Doha—and the Science and Technology Park, home to international and Qatari businesses involved in technology development. But most of these challenges are longer-term. QNRF must keep them in mind and manage them as it evolves.

QNRF will facilitate the growth of Qatar's human capital and help build a national infrastructure that promotes cutting-edge, collaborative research. The RQPI team's recommendations are carefully designed to enable Qatar to meet national needs, benefit its citizens, and take its place among the best of the international centers of research springing up around the world in the global era.

Acknowledgments

The RQPI project team would like to thank Her Highness Sheikha Mozah Bint Nasser Al-Missned and the Qatar Foundation board for the opportunity to conduct this project. We were guided by the leadership of Abdulla al-Kubaisi and Fathy Saoud. We enjoyed and learned from our several discussions with each of them. We also would like to thank Jim McNail, Bill Duffett, Winnie Gonzalves, and Sally Kennedy for their assistance.

Many individuals in Qatar and abroad graciously made themselves available to members of the RQPI project team for interviews and follow-up correspondence. These individuals include members of the Qatar Foundation board, leaders in Education City institutions, prospective tenants of the Science and Technology Park, researchers at Qatar University, government officials, and business leaders. A full listing of our contacts is provided in an appendix of the implementation plan.

We would like to acknowledge the contributions of our RQPI and RAND colleagues. The project team is indebted to C. Richard Neu, original director of RQPI, for his insights and guidance throughout the project. Lulwa al-Thani provided valuable research assistance on other research enterprises in the region. RQPI staff members Donna Betancourt, Joji Montelibano, and Nermin El-Mongi helped to make our visits to Doha smooth and productive. RAND colleague Philip Anton provided valuable research and organizational support early in the project. Throughout the project, communication analyst Susan Bohandy played a valuable role in helping the project team organize and prepare briefings and documents; Stephen Bloodsworth ably assisted the team on various document production issues.

Finally, special thanks are due to two individuals: Lisa Sheldone for her vigilance and superb organizational skills as project manager and Adrienn Lanczos for her excellent and always timely administrative support.

Abbreviations

BDA	Bayh-Dole Act
BES	Basic Energy Sciences
CEP	Center for Effective Philanthropy
CMU	Carnegie Mellon University
DARPA	Defense Advanced Research Projects Agency
DoD	U.S. Department of Defense
DOE	U.S. Department of Energy
E&P	exploration and production
EADS	European Aeronautic Defence and Space Company
EISC	Sub-Committee on Entrepreneurship and Internationalisation
ERC	Economic Review Committee
FRST	Foundation for Research, Science, and Technology
GCC	Cooperation Council for the Arab States of the Gulf
GLT	Global Leaders for Tomorrow
GOIC	Gulf Organization for Industrial Consulting
IP	intellectual property
IPR	intellectual property right
KACST	King Abdulaziz City for Science and Technology
MSFHR	Michael Smith Foundation for Health Research
NIH	National Institutes of Health
NSF	National Science Foundation
NYSTAR	New York State Foundation for Science, Technology, and Innovation
PFR	publicly funded research

PRO	public research organizations
QNRF	Qatar National Research Fund
QSTP	Qatar Science and Technology Park
RAC	research advisory council
REU	Research Experiences for Undergraduates
RFP	request for proposals
Rospatent	Federal Service for Intellectual Property, Patents, and Trademarks
RQPI	RAND-Qatar Policy Institute
RS&T	research, science, and technology
RWJF	Robert Wood Johnson Foundation
S&E	science and engineering
S&T	science and technology
SARC	Scientific and Applied Research Center
SFI	Science Foundation Ireland
UROP	Undergraduate Research Opportunities Program
VCU	Virginia Commonwealth University
WEF	World Economic Forum

CHAPTER ONE

Introduction

Qatar is a small nation, covering slightly less area than Connecticut does and supporting a population of about 840,000, with substantial opportunities to expand its economy, improve the quality of life for its people, and influence regional progress. Possessing an extraordinary base of natural gas and oil reserves, Qatar has the potential to chart its own course over the decades to come, relying more on the spirit of its people and cultivating its own intellectual resources—and those of others—to fuel social progress and sustained development. In the early twenty-first century, the creation of a national research fund is one of several critical steps that Qatar could take to fulfill its potential and meet these aspirations.

Recognizing the need for nationally oriented research, the Qatar Foundation for Education, Science, and Community Development asked the RAND-Qatar Policy Institute (RQPI) to assist in the establishment of the Qatar National Research Fund (QNRF).[1] The Qatar Foundation set forth an ambitious vision of research and its benefits, envisioning research as a catalyst for expanding and diversifying the country's economy; enhancing the education of its citizens and the training of its workforce; and fostering improvements in the health, well being, environment, and security of its own people and those of the region. In striving toward this vision, the Qatar Foundation intended that Qatar would distinguish itself within the region and world as a cosmopolitan nation that embraces scholarly excellence, innovation, creativity, inclusiveness, and merit.

This report explains the approach that the RQPI project team took in responding to the Qatar Foundation's request, presents an overview of the project team's core recommendations, and describes two major outcomes of the project, the business and implementation plans.

Approach

The Qatar Foundation asked RQPI to recommend a design for QNRF and draft business and implementation plans to support its establishment. Reflecting the importance assigned to the effort, the Qatar Foundation called for project completion within six months.

The RQPI project team began by meeting with the Qatar Foundation to develop a preliminary understanding of the proposed fund's vision, mission, goals, and operating principles, which it then refined in a time-compressed analytical process. The project team adopted a two-

---

[1] The Qatar Foundation was established in 1995 "to prepare the people of Qatar and the region to meet the challenges of an ever-changing world, and to make Qatar a leader in innovative education and research." See Qatar Foundation (2007).

pronged, simultaneous, and sometimes iterative approach to support this effort. The project team

- examined various research funding organizations and intellectual property right (IPR) regimes in the United States and other countries as possible models for QNRF.
- consulted numerous individuals in Qatar and elsewhere about the current status of research activities in Qatar, national needs for research, and opportunities and constraints that the Qatar Foundation could face as it implemented its vision.

Comparative Analyses

The RQPI project team conducted a comparative analysis, building on a review of research-based public and private foundations and programs in the United States, Canada, Europe, New Zealand, and the Arabian Gulf[2] region, supplemented by findings from recent reports on foundation effectiveness.[3] The team also drew on its own considerable and varied knowledge and experience of research funding organizations. Indeed, a prerequisite for selection of team members was expertise or direct experience in one or more key research organizations.

The project team reviewed the foundations and programs to improve its understanding of the ways in which research-based institutions develop and implement organizational structures and governance principles, award processes and funding mechanisms, monitoring and evaluation processes, and approaches to institutional planning and growth. Absent formal performance ratings across institutions, one cannot claim that a particular method "works best." However, when the preponderance of institutions operates in a particular way or is moving in a particular direction, it may be reasonable to infer that a particular method has proven successful or, at the very least, "works." On this basis and with supplemental findings from recent reports on foundations' organizational structures, governance principles, and operations, the project team provided recommendations for QNRF.

The project team looked at foundations and programs with commonalities in one or more defining characteristics—e.g., mission and goals, size, age, and financing mechanisms—with the proposed QNRF, for insight into options for design and implementation. No one foundation or program offered a precise analogy to the proposed QNRF, but a range covered many important features.

Table 1.1 lists the most directly comparable and interesting institutions in three categories.[4]

NIH, NSF, and some of the other foundations and programs are significantly larger than the proposed QNRF is expected to be, even over the longer term; nevertheless, they share some common institutional features and offer important insight to research management.

---

[2]   *Arabian Gulf* is the name used here for the body of water that some readers may call the *Persian Gulf*.

[3]   The institutional review draws largely from material found on each of the foundation or program's Web sites, including their strategic plans and annual reports.

[4]   Given the simultaneous and sometimes iterative nature of this analysis, the list with which the RQPI project team started was not the list with which it finished. Some institutions that appeared to be directly comparable and interesting at the outset became less so as the project progressed—and vice versa.

Table 1.1
Comparable Institutions

Category	Institution	Location
U.S. public research organizations	National Institutes of Health (NIH)	United States
	National Science Foundation (NSF)	United States
	NSF Research Experiences for Undergraduates (REU) program	United States
Private foundations and programs	Alfred P. Sloan Foundation	United States
	Massachusetts Institute of Technology's Undergraduate Research Opportunities Program (UROP)	United States
	Michael Smith Foundation for Health Research (MSFHR)	Canada
	Robert Wood Johnson Foundation (RWJF)	United States
Other national models	Foundation for Research, Science, and Technology (FRST)	New Zealand
	King Abdulaziz City for Science and Technology (KACST)	Saudi Arabia
	Science Foundation Ireland (SFI)	Ireland

In addition to the 10 institutions listed in Table 1.1, the project team found a set of foundations and programs that displayed fewer points of commonality with QNRF in terms of overall mission, goals, or approach but that did display a particular feature of interest. These institutions include

- Bill and Melinda Gates Foundation, United States
- Carnegie Corporation of New York, United States
- Defense Advanced Research Projects Agency (DARPA), the central research and development organization for the U.S. Department of Defense (DoD)
- New York State Foundation for Science, Technology, and Innovation (NYSTAR), United States
- U.S. Department of Energy's (DOE's) Basic Energy Sciences (BES) program.

For insight, the project team looked at each of the selected institutions' organizational structure and governance principles, award processes and funding mechanisms, monitoring and evaluation processes, and approaches to planning and growth. For a summary of the findings of the comparative analysis, see Appendix A.

Proceeding simultaneously with the conduct of the comparative analysis and the consultation process, the RQPI team also conducted an analysis of alternative models for managing IPRs. The analysis (for results, see Appendix B) began with an exposition of the key trade-offs that any nation faces when choosing an IPR regime. With these underlying trade-offs in mind, we then identified a number of candidate "models" or templates that QNRF may wish to consider in crafting its own IPR allocation policy. While these models are far from exhaustive, we believe that each is at least a plausible candidate. Moreover, each navigates to a slightly different point in managing implicit policy concerns that we believed to be relevant to Qatar.

Consultations

In conducting the analysis, the RQPI project team consulted numerous individuals in Qatar and abroad about the current status of research activities in Qatar, national needs for research, and opportunities and constraints that QNRF would face. The project team elicited the views and opinions of representatives of the following educational institutions, business enterprises, government institutions, and nongovernmental and international organizations:

- Educational institutions
  - Carnegie Mellon University (CMU)
  - Texas A&M University
  - Qatar University and its Scientific and Applied Research Center (SARC)
  - Virginia Commonwealth University (VCU)
  - Weill Medical College of Cornell University
- Business enterprises
  - Al Fardan Group of Companies
  - Commercial Bank of Qatar
  - European Aeronautic Defence and Space Company (EADS)
  - Exxon Mobil Corporation
  - Gulf Organization for Industrial Consulting (GOIC)
  - Microsoft Corporation
  - Qatar Chamber of Commerce and Industry
  - Qatar Petroleum
  - Qatar Science and Technology Park (QSTP)
  - Shell International
  - Total Exploration and Production (E&P) Qatar
- Qatari government institutions
  - Ministry of Economy and Commerce
  - Ministry of Finance
  - Planning Council
- Nongovernmental and international organizations
  - Qatar Scientific Club.

The Need for a National Research Fund

Through discussions with leaders in business, government, and academia in Qatar as well as with Qatar Foundation board members and staff, the RQPI project team identified a number of national needs that research could help meet. While opinions may vary on how to set priorities among these needs, several stand out, such as these:

- Improving the quality of primary, secondary, and higher education in Qatar and equipping Qatari men and women with the skills needed to thrive in a progressive twenty-first-century economy. Research could explore the impacts of major educational reforms and the relative effectiveness of various teaching methods and materials in an Arabic-language setting.

- Diversifying the economy of Qatar to broaden its base and lessen dependence on a single industrial sector. Research in a wide range of areas would identify new technologies and business opportunities and chart out ways to exploit them.
- Drawing more women into the workforce to enrich their own lives and provide the added value of their skilled labor to the economy. Research could explore the possible mechanisms and social and economic consequences of such a transformation.

Research Needs and Opportunities

Research needs derive from national needs and aspirations for which improved or increased knowledge is required for their fulfillment. In contrast, research opportunities represent lines of inquiry for which Qatar is particularly well suited and has a competitive advantage in attracting researchers from abroad. Such research opportunities need not contribute to national needs (although ideally they would). However, they should contribute to the international visibility of Qatar's efforts and distinguish Qatar as a unique venue for particular areas of research.

What Is Meant by "Research"?

The vision of QNRF requires that its funding activities strive to establish a method or style of thinking that can be broadly instilled in students and staff who are part of the research infrastructure of Qatar. The fundamental attributes of this style of thinking are the ability to identify and formulate problems, understand prior related work, and critically evaluate hypotheses and theses, with particular emphasis on scientific methods. This should be contrasted with a narrower definition of research that answers an externally posed question.

The public and private sectors of Qatar already undertake research in this narrower sense of the word. These sectors are routinely confronted with problems that require research to find a solution. Typically, such research is undertaken with a tender because it is highly specialized or the sponsoring organization lacks in-house resources to answer the question. Often, an external review of the results is required to build confidence in the quality of the answer and to ensure that the answer is feasible in the context of Qatar and the region.

The goal of QNRF is to create an environment in which Qataris can learn how to identify questions that ought to be asked, apply discipline-specific methodologies to answer questions, and evaluate the research results of others. This will increase the national capacity both to answer research questions and to critically evaluate the results of contracted work.

Potential Beneficiaries of Qatar National Research Fund–Sponsored Research and Others with an Interest

Who are QNRF's stakeholders? Stakeholders have an interest in QNRF's operations and effects. They are institutions or individuals funding research, playing a significant role in identifying national needs, competing for funding, potentially benefiting from research results (i.e., entities that can use or act on a research result), or overseeing the distribution of research funds. These stakeholders will help establish the scope for viewpoints that the QNRF board, management, and staff should solicit.

The government of Qatar will play a central role in identifying national needs that might benefit from research sponsored by QNRF. However, it is not the only voice that can speak to Qatar's needs. Private-sector actors are also in a position to express views about national requirements. For example, the banking and finance sectors in Qatar could converge on a research agenda to strengthen their competitive advantage in the global marketplace and request that QNRF solicit proposals and fund research to support such an agenda. Ultimately, the established researcher community of Qatar may also play a significant role.

Clearly, Qatari society is intended to be the primary ultimate beneficiary of QNRF funding. This benefit is broad based and is expected to result in long-term benefits to Qatar. Other beneficiaries will be Qatari institutions that can profit from near-term research results. These institutions include the international corporations operating in Qatar, the private-sector organizations of Qatar (including those with significant government ownership), and government institutions. QNRF seeks input from these nearer-term beneficiaries. This input will help QNRF to evaluate the quality of the research and the success of mechanisms intended to cause results to have an impact on Qatar. These same discussions will also serve to elicit ideas for refined or revised research directions that can be used to shape funding approaches. In the longer term, Qatar-based institutions, such as those in Education City[5] or Qatar University, may play a role in devising ways to measure the long-term changes in Qatar that can be attributed to its research investments.

Finally, it will be essential that stakeholders who provide funds and represent focal points for the expression of national needs will need to participate in the oversight of the QNRF.

Qatar's Research Environment and Challenges

Myriad existing and planned institutions and establishments are helping to shape Qatar's research environment, particularly its infrastructure, among them, Qatar University, the current and anticipated residents of Education City and QSTP, and other public- and private-sector entities. And, while a solid research infrastructure is essential, the research environment also consists of less tangible elements, some of which relate to the nature of the infrastructure, including access to cutting-edge knowledge and the overall quality of collegial interactions. More generally, for Qatar to successfully compete in the international market for researchers, it needs to create an environment conducive to research. This means building a truly cosmopolitan research community with shared research values.

Research in Qatar faces a number of significant challenges relating to the research environment. The Qatar Foundation's investments in Education City and QSTP address some of these. The challenges of creating and sustaining a competitive research community in Qatar, particularly one focused on national needs, can be summarized as follows:

---

[5] Education City is a community of institutions—from kindergarten through postgraduate studies—contributing to education in Qatar and the Arabian Gulf region. The universities in Education City now include Weill Medical College of Cornell University, Texas A&M University, CMU, VCU, and Georgetown University. More universities are expected to come into Education City over the next several years.

- Sustainability
  - How can competitive research programs in science and engineering be created and sustained with only undergraduate degree programs providing the initial local cohort of students who might participate in research?
  - How can undergraduates be incorporated into research programs to create future generations of Qataris who understand and value the contributions research can make in Qatar?
- Continuity
  - How can long-term research programs that benefit Qatar be created and sustained in the face of faculty turnover?
  - How can the disruption to an ongoing research program, caused by relocating a faculty member to Qatar, be minimized?
- Collaboration
  - How can Education City and Qatar University faculty and QSTP research staff be encouraged to collaborate to create self-sustaining programs of research and increased opportunities for undergraduate research projects?
  - How can interaction and collaboration among institutions (i.e., university-university, university-industry, industry-government, and university-government) be fostered to create a research community in Qatar?
  - How can public- and private-sector awareness of the potential benefits of research be improved, and how are opportunities for collaboration best brokered?
- Focus on national interests
  - How can awareness of national needs and private-sector needs be created and sustained among faculty and QSTP research staff, given the turnover of staff?
- Geographic separation
  - How can the isolation of Qatar from the world's research centers be reduced to increase Qatar visibility and draw upon the world's resources for collaboration?
  - How can the effects of the physical separation of Education City and QSTP from Qatar University and the nexus of Qatar's public and private sectors be reduced to encourage interaction?

The central task for the RQPI project team was to identify a series of activities and programs that QNRF could fruitfully pursue to meet these challenges and research needs. We briefly elaborate on these potential funding activities in the following section. We also briefly describe an approach to program evaluation that would enable QNRF to measure success in achieving its goals.

How This Report Is Organized

This report proceeds as follows: Chapter Two presents an overview of the project team's core recommendations, deriving from the comparative analysis and the consultation process; Chapter Three describes two major outcomes of the project, the business and implementation plans; Chapter Four presents concluding observations about QNRF's prospects. Appendix A presents a summary of findings from the comparative analysis; and Appendix B presents an analysis of options for addressing IPRs.

CHAPTER TWO

Core Recommendations

This chapter summarizes the core recommendations that RQPI made to the Qatar Foundation. Recommendations on the structure and function of QNRF flowed from the vision and mission of QNRF, as set by the Qatar Foundation, and the research needs and opportunities in Qatar at this time in its history. That is, the approach that RQPI took was to assess research needs and Qatar's research environment and identify the challenges that QNRF was likely to face. These insights then determined critical functional needs, which, in turn, drove recommendations on organizational structure and operations.

Some of the underlying recommendations found in the business and implementation plans include proprietary information. For that reason, not all of the material associated with these recommendations and found in the plans has been included here.

Mission and Goals

QNRF will be the leading institution in Qatar dedicated to funding research in the national interest. It will address priority economic and social needs and pursue opportunities to attract internationally recognized researchers to study topics of regional and global importance. No other institution currently fills this role.

Vision
The Qatar Foundation envisions research as a catalyst for expanding and diversifying the country's economy; enhancing the education of its citizens and the training of its workforce; and fostering improvements in the health, well being, environment, and security of its own people and those of the region.

Mission
QNRF will advance knowledge and education by supporting original, competitively selected research in the physical, life, and social sciences; engineering and technology; the arts; and humanities. It will provide opportunities for researchers at all levels, from students to professionals, in the private, public, and academic sectors.

To accomplish its mission, QNRF will need a strategy that evolves over time as the human capital for research develops and the infrastructure to support research grows. Figure 2.1 shows this evolving strategy.

Figure 2.1
Qatar National Research Fund's Strategy Evolves in Three Overlapping Phases

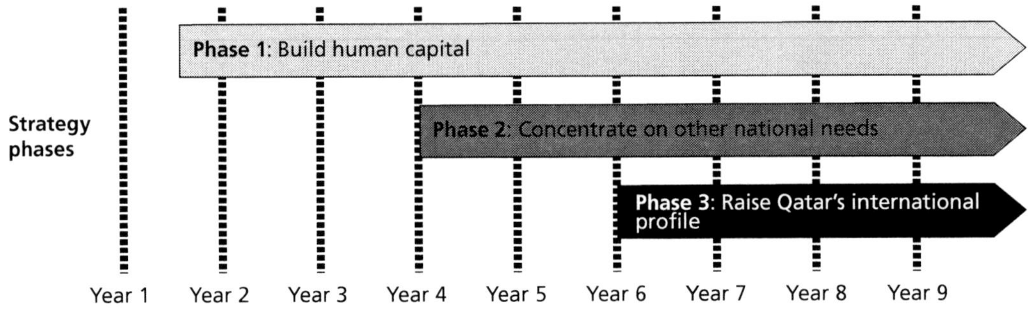

RAND *TR209-2.1*

Goals

To support the first phase of its strategy, QNRF will focus primarily on goals related to building human capital. To support the second and third phases, goals related to other national needs and opportunities, expansion of non-QNRF funding, and raising Qatar's profile in the international research community have been emphasized, as has a continued commitment to the goals for building human capital. The implementation plan suggests specific measures of these goals.

Build Human Capital. A growing number of Education City and Qatar University graduates, medical students, and residents is receiving high-quality education and training in basic and applied research methods. A growing number of researchers in Education City, Qatar University, and firms doing business in Qatar is producing high-quality research products of relevance to Qatar's needs and interests. A growing number of researchers is undertaking multiyear projects. Collaboration is increasing among researchers based in Qatar (from Education City, Qatar University, government, and the private sector). Contacts and collaborations are growing between researchers based in Qatar and the international research community.

More Concentrated Focus on Other National Needs. As a research-oriented institution, QNRF will have limited control over economic performance, environmental quality, public health, and other broad societal outcomes; however, it can aim to contribute through its programs to

- an increase in the number of Qatari men and women holding positions of leadership in Qatar's businesses, universities, and research institutes
- an increase in workforce participation by Qatari women
- an increase in economic diversification in Qatar
- improvements in economic performance through adoption of advanced technologies and best practices among Qatari businesses
- improvements in environmental quality and natural-resource management, in such areas of concern as Arabian Gulf pollution and freshwater supplies
- better health and longer life spans among Qataris
- an increase in the number of Qataris pursuing scholarly and artistic interests, both professionally and for their own personal fulfillment.

Raise Qatar's International Profile in Research and Expand Non-QNRF Funding. Qatar is building a regional and international reputation for its excellence in several research areas. Private-sector sources are voluntarily providing an increasing share of research funding.

The implementation plan suggests specific measures of QNRF's progress in meeting these goals.

Operating Principles

QNRF's operating principles reflect the values of the Qatar Foundation. They will enable the fund to achieve its goals and meet the challenges of the research environment in Qatar.

Service to Qatar
QNRF will serve the people of Qatar as well as its business, academic, and government sectors. It will strive to be a bridge-builder among business, government, academic, and other sectors in Qatar and between Qatar and the international research community. These connections will increase the overall productivity and sharpen the focus of research on Qatar's needs as well as help attract distinguished researchers from abroad.

Problem-Solving and Knowledge Creation
QNRF-supported research will have the overarching purpose of yielding economic, health, social, environmental, and intellectual value to Qatar. Although most of the illustrative research needs identified in the business plan lean heavily in the direction of applied research, *basic research*, defined as the pursuit of knowledge without regard to its application or util- ity, also belongs in QNRF's research portfolio. Indeed, the researchers who engage in basic research will be valuable resources for their more applied colleagues and important mentors and teachers of undergraduates.

Collaboration and Continuity
QNRF will fund programs and projects conducted by a broad array of groups and individuals from universities, businesses, and other sectors. Collaboration among researchers in Qatar and international colleagues will be encouraged. Those conducting research in Qatar will include an international mix of senior, midcareer, and younger researchers from academia, industry, government, and nongovernmental organizations; adjunct faculty from government or indus- try; postdoctoral researchers; graduate students from abroad (initially); and undergraduates and eventually graduate students from universities in Qatar.

Special emphasis will be placed on multi-investigator, multiyear research programs. To the extent possible, QNRF will seek to fund research as part of a coherent research program and, in the absence of a compelling national need, minimize funding of single-investigator projects with little prospect of being sustained by others over time.

Identifiable National Benefits
All QNRF-supported work must have the potential to yield identifiable benefits to Qatar that would be foregone otherwise. QNRF will not duplicate funding of research activities already planned or provided through other arrangements in Education City and QSTP, except in those cases in which such research activities would provide a check or balance on undertakings

that address national priorities. QNRF will conduct workshops and discussions that help it to identify and frame national issues that could be addressed with research programs; survey research results derived from QNRF itself, Education City, and QSTP; and other public and private investments in research.

Merit-Based Research Awards

QNRF-sponsored research will be competitive. QNRF will conduct peer review on all incoming proposals, drawing on an international cadre of researchers. Peer reviewers will evaluate prospective research activities based on (1) the technical merit and creative content of the proposals, (2) the structure and sustainability of the research teams, and (3) the responsiveness of the proposals to the strategic goals of QNRF. QNRF will provide written guidance for these criteria.

Technical merit will be a necessary condition for QNRF sponsorship. Competitive proposals will then be ranked, based on points (2) and (3), i.e., the structure and sustainability of the research teams and the responsiveness of the proposals to the strategic goals of QNRF. Peer reviewers will evaluate the merit of proposals on all three counts. QNRF staff will make the final determinations, considering the assessments of the peer reviewers and the availability of adequate funds to support the research.

Efficiency, Skill, and Breadth

QNRF will operate with as small a staff as possible, focusing resources on research and related support activities, with minimal administrative costs. QNRF will also seek to limit the administrative burdens it imposes on funding recipients and collaborators.

QNRF staff will be professionals with advanced training and research experience in each of the following broad areas: the physical, life, and social sciences; engineering and technology; and the arts and humanities. QNRF staff will draw on an international network of advisors and peer reviewers who can help to evaluate proposals and research results and leading individuals who might be interested in distinguished fellowships affiliated with Qatar University or one of the institutions in Education City. QNRF staff will maintain an awareness of national needs and articulate a work plan and budget for QNRF, manage the merit-based review of proposals, develop and administer contracts, raise funds as required, and work actively to shape research proposals that meet QNRF's research priorities.

Active Publication, Promotion, and Outreach

QNRF will play a significant role in promoting Qatar's research activities, both internally and internationally. This will require QNRF to publish, archive, and summarize research results. It will also require QNRF to broker interactions among the various segments of Qatar's research community (e.g., Qatar University, Education City, QSTP) and between this research community and the public and private sectors of Qatar.

Clearly Defined Intellectual Property Rights

QNRF will manage IPRs in a manner that strikes an appropriate balance between its desire to attract researchers and stimulate innovation yet still advance Qatar's economic interests. A comparative analysis of alternative models for managing IPRs is summarized in a following section and presented in detail in Appendix B.

Funding Activities

QNRF will fund a range of programs and other activities intended to address the needs, opportunities, and challenges identified in the business plan. QNRF's program slate will expand in the first three years of operations, as shown in Figure 2.2.

National Priorities Research Program

The National Priorities Research Program will be the largest funding activity of QNRF and the primary means by which QNRF addresses key national needs through research and pursues research opportunities for which Qatar may have a comparative advantage. Following extensive consultations with business, government, academic, and other leaders, QNRF will articulate several priority research areas and funding strategies, and then solicit for and work interactively with researchers in the appropriate fields to develop primarily multiyear, multi-investigator grant proposals. The program will consist primarily of groupings of integrated and interlocking individual projects. Teams of researchers and groupings of projects may come from a single institution or involve multiple institutions and may span academe and industry.

Criteria for Selecting Priority Research Areas. The selection of priority research areas will be a periodic task undertaken by the director and the governing board, with input from other QNRF staff (e.g., program officers) and the advisory council. Each priority research area will meet at least one of two criteria:

1. The research addresses questions pertinent to the fulfillment of one or more national needs or aspirations, as reflected in QNRF's goals.
2. The research can be shown to open or more fully develop opportunities in which Qatar has a comparative advantage in attracting highly qualified researchers and yielding broadly valued results, also as reflected in QNRF's goals.

In applying the first criterion, QNRF will articulate what constitutes national needs or aspirations. It will have gained understanding of these through extensive consultations with leaders in Qatar, through the QNRF advisory council, and others. Then, QNRF will connect

Figure 2.2
Timeline for Introduction of Qatar National Research Fund Programs and Activities

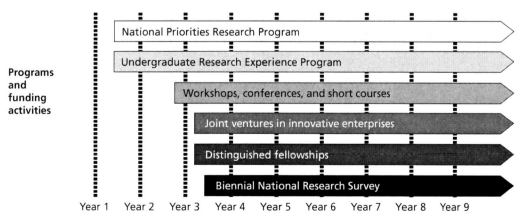

national needs and aspirations to a research agenda. To this end, QNRF will seek research that could lead to better understanding of the need itself, contribute to a knowledge base of how the need manifests itself in Qatar, or lead to a method or solution that could lead to fulfillment of the need.

In applying the second criterion, QNRF will seek to leverage Qatar's national attributes to attract world-class researchers to Qatar. These attributes may include Qatar's labor force demographics, environment, and regional position.

Potential Research Areas to Leverage Opportunities. One of the most important goals of QNRF is to improve Qatar's standing as a place where internationally recognized researchers want to do research on topics of regional and global importance. The RQPI project team identified the following examples of national needs to which research could be productively applied:

- Developing gas and oil resources
- Diversifying the economy
- Improving environmental quality
- Improving the health of Qataris
- Improving water management
- Expanding participation of women in the workplace
- Improving economic performance through adoption of advanced technologies and best practices.

These are some examples of regionally and globally important research areas:

- Educational reform
- Social transformation, particularly the changing role of women
- Genomics
- Marine biology in highly saline waters.

Undergraduate Research Experience Program

QNRF will stimulate undergraduate research opportunities in Education City and Qatar University through individual and group projects led by faculty and other researchers. This will supplement existing programs and contribute to workforce training and wider participation of women in the economy, by funding activities above and beyond those available through ordinary coursework during the academic year. QNRF will solicit proposals from Qatar's academic institutions.

Workshops, Conferences, and Short Courses

These activities, which will occur in Qatar, will include domestic and international participants. Workshops, conferences, and short courses will help to connect researchers in Qatar to their colleagues abroad, as well as attract and inform scientists from abroad about research and other opportunities in Qatar. Also through workshops and informal discussions, QNRF will actively engage researchers and government and business leaders based in Qatar to encourage collaboration and build a sense of common purpose within the country.

Joint Ventures in Innovative Enterprises

QNRF will consider proposals to partner with a university, firm, or individual in Qatar to pursue applied research in a particularly promising area with a goal of commercialization. This activity will fund, in whole or in part, innovative enterprises and related research. Each project will require at least one Qatari partner.

Distinguished Fellowships

These grants will support internationally known researchers and distinguished individuals in the physical, life, and social sciences and the arts and humanities to reside in Qatar for several months to a year so that they may share their expertise and talent with the Qatar community.

Biennial National Research Survey

Every other year, QNRF will publish a summary of all research conducted in Qatar. This summary will serve as the national repository of all data-collection efforts, findings, and scientific and technical publications.

Extension Service

In the future, the QNRF may wish to consider providing an extension service to help Qatar's industries and government apply research results generated by the Qatar Foundation's investments in Education City, QSTP, and QNRF.

Intellectual Property Rights

QNRF aspires to encourage and maintain an active research environment. If it succeeds, inventions and creative works with appreciable market potential may result. According to the implementation plan, QNRF's governing board will choose the most appropriate approach to IPRs during its first meeting. The business plan recommends that QNRF adopt a policy in which grant recipients ("grantees") retain IPRs.

The plan recommends that the approach strike a balance among a number of important considerations:

- QNRF should finalize and clearly articulate its IPR policy prior to the launch of operations, with a transparent framework for any exceptions or exclusions.
- The approach should reflect QNRF's overarching goal to benefit the people of Qatar and the region, not to function as a conduit for Qatari financing of research commercialized abroad.
- Most nations appear to be converging on an international IPR model similar to what has been prevalent in the United States since 1980. This approach presumptively assigns rights to grantees (with some restrictions). While small deviations from the emerging international standard are unlikely to hamper QNRF's effectiveness, significant deviations—particularly if coupled with less protection for grantees—could drive away researchers from abroad.

- The underlying system should remain sufficiently flexible to allow for tailoring in individual cases, conferring lesser or greater degrees of protection to certain grantees when circumstances require.

Table 2.1 compares four IPR allocation models; Appendix B explores each in considerably more detail. Under the fund ownership model, QNRF would maintain default control over IPRs. Under the joint ownership model, ownership would be explicitly divided between QNRF and the grantee. Under the prevailing international model, the grantee would maintain default control over IPRs. Finally, under the Canadian model, the grantee would enjoy the benefit of a general policy preference favoring grantee ownership, but the approach would allow QNRF slightly greater flexibility—and less of an administrative burden—in declaring an exception to exist. Under each proposed model, the allocation of IPRs could be changed through an express contract between QNRF and the grantee. On all other criteria, however, the various models differ from one another.

The business plan concludes that either the prevailing international or Canadian model would strike an acceptable balance for QNRF. The prevailing international model would vest slightly greater power in the hands of grantees than would the Canadian model. Further, the prevailing international model is likely better known and understood by grantees throughout the world and could make Qatar more attractive as a place to conduct research. The Canadian model, however, would offer an administrative advantage to QNRF by making it easier for it to exercise its rights when clearly in the national interest. This option still captures the advantages of commonality with most other nations and substantially preserves the incentives to innovate offered by the prevailing international model. While Canada has chosen to implement its approach through an administrative policy framework, Qatar could incorporate similar provisions in law for use by QNRF and other funders. The ultimate choice between these two models should be based on further analysis of (1) Qatar's ability to attract distinguished researchers under a Canadian model that deviates, however slightly, from the prevailing international model and (2) the nature and extent of circumstances in which QNRF would seek to exercise its rights. If the Canadian model—implemented through law rather than policy—is indeed viewed as an excessive deterrent to attracting researchers, then it should not be pursued. This is an issue of marketing, not law. On the other hand, if the Qatar Foundation and QNRF perceive that protecting the rights that concern the national interest are

Table 2.1
Summary of Alternative Models for Intellectual Property Rights

Model	Description
Fund ownership	QNRF retains all IPRs and rights to license to third parties.
Joint ownership	Each party (grantee and QNRF) assumes 50% undivided interest in IPRs.
Prevailing international approach	By legal *presumption*, grantee retains IPRs and rights to license. If QNRF declares an exception or asserts its discretion to take over ("march in") rights from the grantee and the grantee appeals, *QNRF* must demonstrate the basis for its decision.
Canadian approach	QNRF formally retains IPRs but adopts a stated policy that favors assignment to grantee in most cases. If QNRF declares an exception or asserts its discretion to take over ("march in") rights from the grantee, the *grantee* must demonstrate that QNRF's decision was arbitrary.

paramount, then opting for a statute-based version of the Canadian model might be most prudent. In addition to these considerations, the choice of model should be informed by a comparative assessment of the transaction costs and administrative burden of the two models.

The plan budgets for legal counsel in Qatar. Qatari law is still not well developed in the areas of copyright and patents, and a local expert in these areas may prove to be an exceptionally useful asset for consultations.

Organizational Structure

We recommend a board-led approach, similar to that of NSF and several other foundations and programs. While it would give the director significant authority to operate the organization, it would draw on a wide base of knowledge, experience, and interest to establish the overall direction of QNRF, set policy, and provide institutional oversight. In addition, QNRF should consider forming one or more advisory committees to provide both expertise and additional links to stakeholders.

Based on both the foundation and program reviews and the recent Center for Effective Philanthropy (CEP) reports (Boston Foundation, 2002; Buchanan, 2004; CEP, 2002a, 2002b), we also recommend an actively engaged board, i.e., one that participates in institutional assessments, brings "thought-provoking and important concerns" to the director's attention, provides "financial and strategic stewardship," and periodically and candidly assesses its own performance. We also discourage micromanagement.

Figure 2.3 shows the proposed organizational structure.

Governing Board
The business plan recommends a six-member governing board that would ensure that QNRF's mission and goals are implemented in a sound and timely manner. The governing board would be accountable to the Qatar Foundation for QNRF's performance.

Director
The director will manage QNRF's day-to-day operations within the policy guidelines that the governing board set. The director will be an ex officio, nonvoting member of the governing board and works with the board on QNRF policy and planning. The director will report to the governing board.

Advisory Council
The QNRF advisory council will be comprised of leaders from Qatar's academic and business communities. It will provide formal and informal advice to the governing board on programmatic questions. The advisory council will be accountable to the board but will not make funding, operational, or policy decisions and will not be empowered to act on behalf of QNRF.

Other Staff
The CFO, program officers, and other staff will manage and implement QNRF programs and other funding activities and operations. They will report to the director. Staff positions can be added incrementally as needed. The director may employ staff or consultants on a part-time basis or share the time of administrative assistants with the Qatar Foundation.

Figure 2.3
Organizational Chart for the Qatar National Research Fund

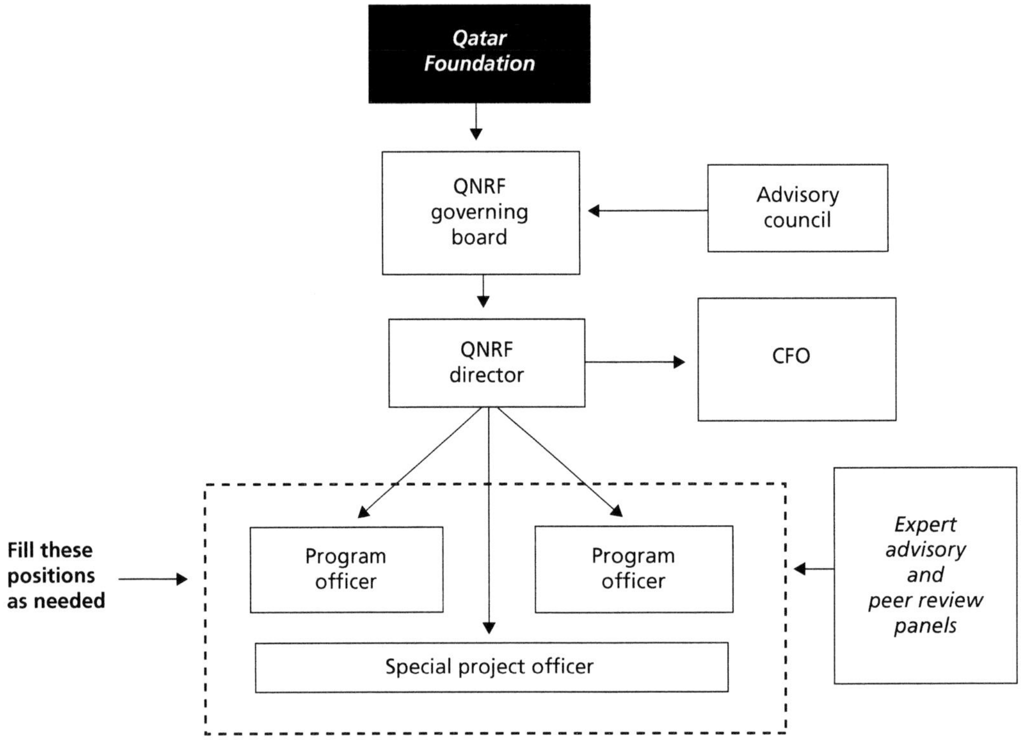

RAND *TR209-2.3*

Requisite Skills of Qatar National Research Fund Management and Staff

The skills of QNRF staff were inferred from an analysis of Qatar's research needs and the preceding recommendations on types of funding activities. They include the following.

- Technical competence
    - Have a Ph.D. in the physical, life, or social sciences; engineering; the arts; or the humanities (for the director and program officers).
    - Have broad knowledge and experience across academic and professional disciplines.
    - Understand the management of basic and applied research.
- Awareness
    - Maintain an awareness of research activities in Qatar's public and private sectors, QSTP, Qatar University, and Education City.
    - Maintain an awareness of Qatar's national research infrastructure's capabilities and capacity.
    - Relate research conducted in Qatar to comparable worldwide research efforts.
    - Maintain an awareness of Qatar's national needs.
    - Be cognizant of research results.

- Leadership
  - Work with the public and private sectors to identify needs that could be met through research and opportunities to host undergraduate research activities,
  - Work with faculty and research staff to shape research proposals,
- Networking and bridge-building
  - Draw on an international network of researchers and institutions that can help evaluate proposals and on leading individuals who might be interested in a role as scholar in residence affiliated with Qatar University or one of the institutions in Education City,
  - Build networks of contacts among researchers and others in Education City, QSTP, and the public and private sectors; broker relationships among contacts,
  - Gather input from stakeholders to build support for a research agenda; articulate the research agenda,
  - Represent Qatar's research community in international forums,
- Advice
  - Advise government and the private sector about the sciences, technology, and the arts and humanities,
- Administration
  - Develop and administer contracts,
  - Produce concise publications to publicize QNRF work,
  - Raise funds from individuals and firms to supplement QNRF activities,
  - Manage finances.

Financial Structure

The business plan identifies the minimal funding level to sustain viable and vital QNRF programs and other funding activities. To finance these activities, the plan compares and contrasts two approaches: an endowment and a pay-as-you-go annual funding scheme.

Funding

Each of the QNRF programs and other funding activities will need some critical mass to be cost-effective and to justify the effort to establish them. Critical mass can be viewed as the engagement of a sufficient number of researchers to contribute to achieving QNRF goals for human capital and other national needs. It also captures the minimal activity to justify fixed administrative costs.

Not all programs can be implemented at full funding in the first year. Some ramp-up time will be required. For example, for the distinguished-fellowship program to be successful, some research infrastructure has to be in place to support the fellows. Allocation of funding in excess of the minimum recommended levels should take into account the maximum capacity of each of the various programs to fruitfully absorb funding. After the initial year, QNRF will use information produced by the evaluation process to help in the fund allocation decision. Fund allocation may also be influenced by the sources of financing for the fund; donors may want to target a particular area rather than simply donate to a general fund or to build up an endowment.

Financing

The choice here is among an endowment, a pay-as-you-go scheme, or a combination of the two. Each of the first two choices has its advantages and disadvantages. Each choice influences fundraising opportunities and has different implications for fundraising strategies.

An endowment is used almost universally by private research organizations like the Alfred P. Sloan Foundation, RWJF, and many others. In most cases, a large initial grant served as the basis of the endowment, which has been supplemented over the years by charitable donations.

The pay-as-you-go scheme is similar to the financing mechanism for NSF and other government-sponsored research organizations throughout the world. NSF, while it may fund multiyear efforts, is financed on an annual basis through an annual government appropriation.

Recommendation

The plan notes the significant advantages of an endowment approach for establishing the long-term orientation of QNRF, as well as the near-term advantages of also providing a mechanism to accept pay-as-you-go funding for special projects as well as QNRF programs generally. Therefore, the plan recommends that both approaches be adopted.

Implementation

We recommend that implementation proceed in three stages: (1) start-up; (2) launch operations and programs; and (3) deepen and broaden the research agenda. Figure 2.4 shows the relative timing of implementation stages with the three strategy phases.

We recommend that the Qatar Foundation's first action in the start-up stage be to name a start-up manager, who would manage the search and selection of members of the governing board, the director, and members of the advisory council. Thereafter, the governing board and director would assume responsibility for the remaining tasks needed to implement QNRF operations and funding activities. The hand-over from the start-up manager to the director would be expected to occur approximately five months after QNRF being established. The implementation plan details the month-by-month milestones that the QNRF board and staff would need to meet to establish a strong organization and subsequently launch funding activities. Figures 2.5 and 2.6 summarize these milestones. The plan further describes the routine QNRF operations subsequent to the start-up and launch of programs.

Award Processes and Funding Mechanisms

We provide recommendations for soliciting proposals, choosing among funding mechanisms, reviewing proposals, and making awards. Details and references supporting these recommendations can be found in Appendix A.

With regard to solicitation, we recommend a combination of two general approaches: (1) consulting with experts in the field, to help identify specific needs in particular research areas, and (2) formulating requests for proposals internally, within QNRF, to help ensure fulfillment of the fund's overarching mission and goals. With regard to undergraduate research, the REU approach, which requires program elements that are specific to the active participation of undergraduate researchers but does not prescribe particular research areas, offers considerable appeal in its generality.

Figure 2.4
Qatar National Research Fund Operations Evolve in Parallel with Strategy Phases

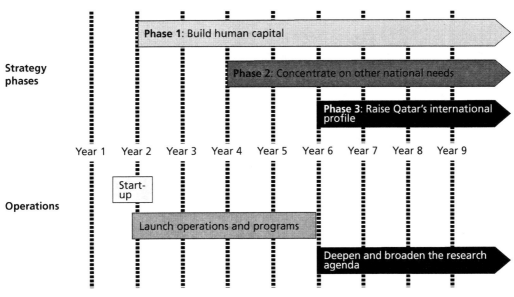

RAND *TR209-2.4*

Figure 2.5
Timeline for the Start-Up of the Qatar National Research Fund: June Through November of Year 1

Phase	Year 1	Who's Responsible	Main Steps
Start-up	June	• Qatar Foundation	• approves business plan • appoints start-up manager.
	July August	• Start-up manager	• begins recruiting the director • begins recruiting board members.
	September	• Qatar Foundation	• incorporates QNRF • establishes legal and financial basis.
		• Start-up manager	• screens candidates for board • screens candidates for director • secures facilities and infrastructure.
	October	• Qatar Foundation	• interviews candidates for director • appoints director • appoints board members • names members of advisory council.
	November	• Director	• begins residence in Doha • initiates consultations about research priorities.

RAND *TR209-2.5*

**Figure 2.6
Timeline for Completion of Start-Up and Launch of Operations and Programs: December of
Year 1 Through September of Year 2**

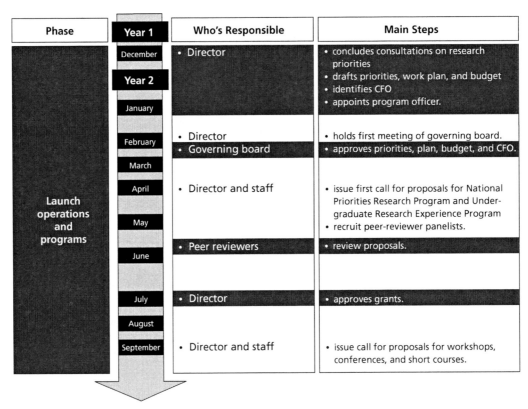

RAND *TR209-2.6*

With regard to funding mechanisms, we recommend a list of clearly defined and structured funding mechanisms similar to that of SFI to allow for simplified and standardized solicitation and selection processes. The list would provide tools for funding different kinds of projects, such as research grants, undergraduate research-based education awards, and workshop and conference grants, each of which would address one or more of the fund's goals.

Regarding selections and award-making, we recommend peer review. Tying funding decisions to a peer-review process would help to establish the fund as a credible research institution, internationally. Both NSF and NIH offer good basic frameworks. Peer review, when combined with a solicitation process and funding mechanisms that emphasize QNRF's strategic goals, would help QNRF credibly address all aspects of its mission.

Monitoring and Evaluation Processes

We provide recommendations for both institutional- and project-level evaluations and monitoring. According to several recent reports (Aspen Institute, 2002; Boston Foundation, 2002; CEP, 2002a, 2002b), the evidence on performance-assessment methods suggests the importance of developing measures of institutional- and project-level impacts, while recognizing the importance of planning processes and operational considerations in generating results. A full multilevel assessment may require a combination of measures, touching on all three areas—impacts, planning, and operations. Moreover, given the amount of effort needed, the evidence also suggests the importance of developing both the measures and an overall assessment system as soon as possible in the life of an institution, with the intent to iterate and adjust practices over time.

Institutional-level evaluation will be crucial, even in the earliest phases of QNRF. A rigorous evaluation of the fund's performance in meeting its goals and furthering its mission is important not only for planning future growth, as addressed below, but also for solidifying its role in the research community in Qatar and maximizing its impact on research worldwide. To promote quality and transparency and better serve Qatar, we also recommend formally incorporating outside views, through surveys or third-party reviews.

As part of its institutional assessment activities, we recommend that QNRF regularly assess the distribution of funding across the entirety of its portfolio, to determine whether the distribution is in line with its mission and goals. To this point, portfolio management indicators might include the following:

- balance between single-year and multiyear QNRF-sponsored programs and projects
- balance between single-investigator and multi-institutional, collaborative QNRF-sponsored programs and projects
- extent of Qatari participation in QNRF-sponsored programs and projects
- extent of international participation in QNRF-sponsored programs and projects
- distribution of funding in relation to national priorities, including economic diversification, technology adoption, local and regional environmental quality, public health, and the participation of Qatari women in the workforce
- distribution of funding across research fields.

Other management indicators might include the following:

- share of programs and projects submitting annual and final progress reports within stated timeframes and deadlines
- share of programs and projects resulting in "closeout" reports
- share of programs and projects represented in project databases.

We also recommend that QNRF work to develop indicators of program and project effectiveness. Project-level monitoring and evaluation are necessary for building a base of consistent, high-quality, and well-documented research support. However, if QNRF supports several funding mechanisms, it may need to tailor its reporting requirements; that is, a research grant, an undergraduate research-based education award, and a workshop or conference grant should have somewhat different reporting requirements. Nevertheless, certain basic requirements should cut across most, if not all, program areas. For example, all award recipients should submit annual and final progress reports on a timely basis. The reports should clearly identify project accomplishments in specific dimensions, such as publications, reports, patents, etc. They should also provide an accurate accounting of the use of funds. QNRF will need this detailed information to assess its performance at a higher, intuitional level. Examples might include the following:

- increased availability of research-based educational opportunities for undergraduates, medical students, and residents

- increased frequency of internationally recognized and attended workshops, conferences, and short courses
- share of QNRF-sponsored programs and projects resulting in publication, reports, patents, or other documented work products, and measures of quality associated with these products
- contributions of QNRF-sponsored programs and projects to the realization of national priorities, including but not limited to economic diversification, technology adoption, improvements in local and regional environmental quality, improvements in public health outcomes, and an increase in the participation of Qatari women in the workforce.

For QNRF to implement some of these indicators, it would need baseline estimates, e.g., current availability of research-based education opportunities, and ongoing project-level tracking.

Conducting a rigorous and thorough review of programs will be essential as the end of QNRF's initial three- to five-year period approaches and management considers scaling up its operation by broadening and deepening programs.

Approaches to Planning and Growth

Several of the selected institutions look to internal evaluation processes, community perceptions, and functional priorities to guide planning. Soliciting views from those affected by QNRF activities will be crucial to determining when and how the fund should expand. In this regard, the approaches to community engagement of several of the organizations we examined, in which they look to stakeholders for guidance, provide appropriate models. However, QNRF should also develop regular processes of self-evaluation, such as those that RWJF uses, as they will provide the necessary information to fine tune—and occasionally substantially modify—the QNRF growth strategy.

Overall, successful expansion will require a clear plan of action, addressing growth in either the depth or breadth of programs and demonstrating alignment with recognized needs.

In conclusion, we note that the call for outside views features prominently in virtually every dimension of institutional planning and operations, ranging from governance to growth. Perhaps one of the most effective ways in which QNRF can remain true to its mission and goals is by actively seeking outside views as soon and regularly as practicable.

CHAPTER THREE

Project Outcomes

At the time of this writing, the Qatar Foundation had made a commitment in principle to implementing QNRF along the lines generally recommended by RQPI in the business and implementation plans. These plans were intended to provide the foundation with a road map for decisionmaking and implementation. The business plan serves as a philosophical document charting the needs, opportunities, and challenges facing QNRF. It also frames and analyzes key business decisions regarding financing and IPRs that the Qatar Foundation will need to make now and in the future as it moves forward with QNRF. The implementation plan is intended to be a manual for Qatar Foundation and QNRF staff as they organize their actions and priorities to stand the organization up and operate it in an efficient manner.

In this chapter, we briefly summarize the content and structure of these essential documents of this project.

Business Plan

The business plan answered key questions about the rationale for QNRF, how it will spend its funds, and whence the funds might come.

The plan was organized to address the following questions:

- Section 1, Introduction: What does QNRF aspire to do? How will it do it?
- Section 2, Research Needs and Opportunities: What are Qatar's potential research needs as it seeks to fulfill its national aspirations? What are potential research opportunities for which Qatar may be uniquely well suited? How will QNRF identify these needs and opportunities in the future? Who are the potential beneficiaries of QNRF-sponsored research in Qatar? How might QNRF approach IPRs?[1]
- Section 3, Qatar's Research Environment and Challenges: Who are the researchers who would conduct research in and for Qatar? What research-related infrastructure is available in Qatar to support research activities? What challenges face QRNF?
- Section 4, Proposed Activities and Requisite Staff Skills: What kinds of activities should QNRF fund to overcome these challenges? What kinds of funding activities would be most effective at meeting QNRF mission and goals? What skills must QNRF staff possess to implement these activities effectively?

---

[1] The discussion of IPRs in the business plan draws on the material in Appendix B of this technical report.

- Section 5, Organizational Structure and Governance: How will QNRF be structured? How will it be governed? What are key roles and responsibilities of the governing board, director, and other staff? How will these match up with the skill sets identified in section 4?
- Section 6, Estimated Costs of Funding Activities and Operations: How much will these types of research and other activities cost? How much will it cost to administer QNRF? What might a budget for QNRF look like?
- Section 7, Options for Funding Mechanisms: From where will QNRF's money come and how should it be managed?
- Section 8, Analysis of the Plan: What are the strengths, weaknesses, risks, and opportunities of the QNRF business plan?

Implementation Plan

The implementation plan was designed to serve as a how-to manual, providing specific guidance to

- the Qatar Foundation in its establishment of QNRF
- QNRF management, staff, and governing board as they start the fund, launch programs, and sustain operations.

Some elements of the business plan are reproduced in the implementation plan to provide easier access for staff that may use this plan on a near-daily basis. Further, some parts of the material contained in the implementation plan may be used to explain QNRF programs and procedures to a broader audience. Not surprisingly, the implementation plan focuses most of its guidance on the first year or two, during QNRF's start-up stage of operations and the subsequent stage of launching operations and programs, as shown in Figure 2.4. Less detail was provided on the latter stages of deepening and broadening QNRF's research agenda.

The implementation plan was organized as follows,

- Concept
  - Section 1, Outline of the Plan: This section outlined the content of the plan and the sequence of actions required to establish QNRF.
  - Section 2, Overview of the QNRF: This section summarized the vision, mission, evolving strategy, goals, funding activities, and implementation of QNRF.
  - Section 3, Organizational Structure and Governance: This section presented the structure and governance of QNRF. The section also described the qualifications, roles, responsibilities, and relationships of key players in the organization.
- Implementing Actions
  - Section 4, Start-Up: Establishing the QNRF: This section presented the first steps the Qatar Foundation and its designated personnel would undertake to initiate the organization of QNRF. These steps would be taken during the project's first 15 months—from June 2004 to September 2005.
  - Section 5, Launching Operations and Programs: This section described the funding activities and the operational tasks needed to launch them after the governing board

and director were selected and in place. These actions would take more than 18 months to complete.

- – Section 6, Running the QNRF: Standard Procedures: This section described the key operational procedures and tasks that need to be undertaken on a regular basis.
- – Section 7, Expanding the QNRF: This section briefly addressed the third phase of QNRF's development and outlined some key issues that QNRF management may wish to consider three to five years after the start-up phase.

- Supporting Materials
  - – Section 8, Reference Materials: This section presented background material, guides, and references that may be consulted in the process of setting up QNRF.
  - – Section 9, Sample Documents: This section presented sample documents, such as job descriptions for QNRF staff, which may be used in the operations and activities of QNRF.

CHAPTER FOUR

Concluding Observations

The business plan was based on numerous assumptions about the *external* environment in which QNRF would operate—most importantly, the research and education community that includes Qatar University, Education City, and QSTP. The business plan was also based on numerous assumptions about the *internal* development of QNRF—namely, its governance structure, organizational capacity, and program designs.

The Qatar Foundation will face strengths, weaknesses, opportunities, and risks if it chooses to establish QNRF. Strengths represent areas in which the proposed QNRF design is likely to ensure that it meets expectations. Weaknesses represent areas in which the QNRF design may cause it to fall short of expectations. Opportunities are directions that could significantly improve QNRF's impact in Qatar. Risks could seriously impair QNRF's ability to meet expectations. Table 4.1 summarizes these.

The business and implementation plans recognize that QNRF will face some surprises and setbacks as it embarks on its ambitious vision. Routine program evaluation will be an essential feature of QNRF operations. Frequent and substantive interactions among QNRF board members, staff, and stakeholders will provide valuable information about the effectiveness and relevance of QNRF activities. With the appropriate data in hand, the QNRF's governing board and staff should be able to recognize when divergence from established plans may be necessary.

Perhaps more than any other single factor, staffing decisions will have a large influence on QNRF success. The QNRF board and staff will need to maintain a laserlike focus on the QNRF mission and goals and resist the temptation to spread their resources too thinly. At the same time, they will need to remain flexible and opportunistic within a rapidly changing

Table 4.1
Assessment of the Qatar National Research Fund's Internal and External Environment

Environment	Strengths or Opportunities	Weaknesses or Risks
Internal	Planned funding base is ample. Planned overhead is modest. Programs designed to meet real needs.	Small staff and ambitious recruiting efforts could lead to schedule delays. The two primary options for financing QNRF have limitations that could adversely affect QNRF programs.
External	QNRF can foster collaboration. QNRF can catalyze the research culture. QNRF can become a community leader. QNRF can create positive, professional relationships within Qatar.	QNRF programs are undersubscribed. Institutional, cultural, and geographic barriers hinder local and international collaboration. Researchers may become dependent on the QNRF. Faculty and research staff may fail to engage undergraduates in research.

environment. This will be a difficult balancing act to maintain. Putting in place a strong staff and organizational foundation will go a long way toward building a strong and sustainable research funding enterprise in Qatar.

Comparative Analysis of Research Funding Organizations

Victoria A. Greenfield and Gabrielle Bloom

Our comparative analysis builds on a review of research-based public and private foundations and programs in the United States, Canada, Europe, New Zealand, and the Arabian Gulf region and is supplemented by findings from recent reports on foundation effectiveness.[1]

We reviewed the foundations and programs to improve our understanding of the ways in which research-based institutions develop and implement organizational structures and governance principles, award processes and funding mechanisms, monitoring and evaluation processes, and approaches to institutional planning and growth. Absent more formal performance ratings across institutions, we cannot claim that a particular method "works best." However, when the preponderance of institutions operates in a particular way or is moving in a particular direction, it may be reasonable to infer that a particular method has proven successful or, at the very least, "works." On this basis and with supplemental findings from recent reports, we provide recommendations for QNRF.

Foundations and Programs

We looked at foundations and programs with commonalities in defining characteristics—e.g., mission, goals, size, age, financing mechanisms, or other operating parameters—with the proposed QNRF, for insight into options for design and implementation. No one foundation or program offers a precise analogy to QNRF, but a range covers many important features.

Here, we list the most directly comparable and interesting institutions alphabetically in three categories, U.S. public research organizations, private foundations and programs, and other national models.

- U.S. public research organizations
    - NIH, owing to its preeminence as a sponsor of health research and education and to its well-established proposal review and assessment processes
    - NSF, owing to its preeminence in the field of science and engineering research and education and to its well-established governance structure and proposal-review and performance-assessment processes
    - REU, owing to its focus on promoting opportunities for undergraduate research, by funding projects at wide-ranging facilities and institutions in disciplinary and interdisciplinary settings

---

[1] The institutional review draws largely from material found on each of the foundation or program's Web sites, including their strategic plans and annual reports.

- Private foundations and programs
  - Alfred P. Sloan Foundation, owing to similarities in fields of interest, including science and technology (S&T) and economic development
  - UROP, owing to its emphasis on undergraduate research-based education
  - MSFHR, owing to similarities in its goals for health research, its size, and its age, i.e., it is a relative newcomer
  - RWJF, owing to its research, training, and education programs in the health arena
- Other national models
  - FRST, owing to its role as the New Zealand government's "principle purchaser of research, science, and technology (RS&T) outputs and manager of RS&T funds" (FRST, 2003b)
  - KACST, owing to similarities in its overall mission and goals
  - SFI, owing to similarities in its overall mission and goals and to its age, i.e., it is a relative newcomer.

NIH, NSF, and some of the other foundations and programs are significantly larger than the proposed QNRF is likely to be, even over the longer term; nevertheless, they share some common institutional features and offer important insight to research management.

In addition to the 10 institutions listed above, we found a set of foundations and programs that displayed fewer points of commonality with QNRF in terms of overall mission, goals, or approach but did display a particular feature of interest. These institutions include

- Bill and Melinda Gates Foundation, owing to its rapid initiation of major projects and its proactive approach to cultivating new projects
- Carnegie Corporation of New York, owing to its grant agreements and the terms it sets for grantees
- DARPA, the central R&D organization for DoD, owing to the interactive approach that it takes with its researchers and to its proactive approach to finding new and promising opportunities in the fields of interest
- NYSTAR, owing to its focus on public-private partnerships and on the economic benefits to be gained from the support of research in the state
- BES, also owing to the interactive approach that it takes with its researchers and to its relationship to the several affiliated national laboratories.

Having identified a pool of foundations and programs for review, we then looked at their organizational structures and governance principles, award processes and funding mechanisms, monitoring and evaluation processes, and approaches to planning and growth for insight. Table A.1 provides information about each of the 15 institutions, including their missions and goals.

Organizational Structures and Governance Principles
Most of the foundations and government programs included in this discussion share the general structure of a governing board or board of trustees functioning as the main decisionmaking body on issues concerning the overall direction of the institution. In some cases, they also make some operational decisions, such as those regarding requests for proposals (RFPs) or awards. For example, the NSF National Science Board establishes agency policies, oversees

Table A.1
Foundations and Programs and Their Missions

Institution	Country	Public/ Private	Mission	Goals
NIH	United States	Public	*The National Institutes of Health is the steward of medical and behavioral research for the Nation. (NIH, 2007a)*	*The goals of the agency are as follows: 1. foster fundamental creative discoveries, innovative research strategies, and their applications as a basis to advance significantly the Nation's capacity to protect and improve health; 2. develop, maintain, and renew scientific human and physical resources that will assure the Nation's capability to prevent disease; 3. expand the knowledge base in medical and associated sciences in order to enhance the Nation's economic well-being and ensure a continued high return on the public investment in research; and 4. exemplify and promote the highest level of scientific integrity, public accountability, and social responsibility in the conduct of science. (NIH, 2007a)*
NSF	United States	Public	*To promote the progress of science; to advance the national health, prosperity, and welfare; to secure the national defense; and for other purposes. (P.L. 81-507)*	***Discovery*** *Foster research that will advance the frontiers of knowledge, emphasizing areas of greatest opportunity and potential benefit and establishing the nation as a global leader in fundamental and transformational science and engineering.* ***Learning*** *Cultivate a world-class, broadly inclusive science and engineering workforce, and expand the scientific literacy of all citizens.* ***Research Infrastructure*** *Build the nation's research capability through critical investments in advanced instrumentation, facilities, cyberinfrastructure and experimental tools.* ***Stewardship*** *Support excellence in science and engineering research and education through a capable and responsive organization. (NSF, 2006b, p. 5)*
REU	United States	Public	*The Research Experiences for Undergraduates (REU) program supports active research participation by undergraduate students in any of the areas of research funded by the National Science Foundation. (NSF, 2007)*	*The REU program seeks to expand student participation in all kinds of research--whether disciplinary, interdisciplinary, or educational in focus--encompassing efforts by individual investigators, groups, centers, national facilities, and others. (NSF, 2006c)*

Table A.1—Continued

Institution	Country	Public/ Private	Mission	Goals
Alfred P. Sloan Foundation	United States	Private	*The Sloan Research Fellowship Program aims to stimulate fundamental research by young scholars with outstanding promise to contribute significantly to the advancement of knowledge.* (Alfred P. Sloan Foundation, 2006)	Goals are program-specific, e.g., *The primary missions of [the Industry Studies] Program are to encourage research cooperation between academics and industry, and to support the integration of observation-based research with appropriate theory and analysis among a growing community of industry studies scholars* (Alfred P. Sloan Foundation, undated[b]).
UROP	United States	Private	Provide undergraduates with rewarding, real-life research experience (see UROP, undated).	Foster mentoring relationships between students and faculty and research staff (see UROP, undated).
MSFHR	Canada	Private	*The Michael Smith Foundation for Health Research leads, partners and serves as a catalyst to build British Columbia's capacity for excellence in clinical, biomedical, health services and population health research.* (MSFHR, 2006).	*As British Columbia's provincially mandated health research organization, the Michael Smith Foundation for Health Research builds BC's capacity for excellence in health research by: 1. leading, partnering and serving as a catalyst to advance provincial, inter-provincial and national initiatives that expand health research support and opportunities; 2. working with health research stakeholders to identify, prioritize and respond to provincial priorities; and 3. delivering innovative programs to address the key building blocks of a vibrant, sustainable research effort.* (MSFHR, 2006)
RWJF	United States	Private	*The Robert Wood Johnson Foundation seeks to improve the health and health care of all Americans.* (RWJF, undated)	*To achieve the most impact with our funds, we prioritize our grants into four goal areas: To assure that all Americans have access to quality health care at reasonable cost. . . . To improve the quality of care and support for people with chronic health conditions. . . . To promote healthy communities and lifestyles. . . . To reduce the personal, social and economic harm caused by substance abuse—tobacco, alcohol and illicit drugs.* (RWJF, undated)
FRST	New Zealand	Public	*We aim to stimulate prosperity and improve the well-being of New Zealanders and the environment through investing in innovation and fostering the creation of new knowledge.* (FRST, undated)	Invest in a wide range of research, science, and technology initiatives with economic, environmental, and social benefits; stimulate both research providers and the users of research to innovate and create knowledge; and work closely with other government agencies to ensure a seamless approach to assisting industry (see FRST, undated).

Table A.1—Continued

Institution	Country	Public/ Private	Mission	Goals
KACST	Saudi Arabia	Public	*From its inception in 1977, KACST had been carrying out its mission in the promotion of science [and] technology in the Kingdom. . . (KACST, undated)*	*. . . by coordinating and cooperating with various universities, agencies and institutions concerned with research and technology, and encouraging Saudi experts to undertake research that will help promote the development and evolution of the society. Besides this, KACST, through cooperative agreements with international science and technology institutions/ organizations, encourages closer ties with friendly countries. (KACST, undated)*
SFI	Ireland	Public	*SFI will build and strengthen scientific and engineering research and its infrastructure in the areas of greatest strategic value to Ireland's long-term competitiveness and development. (SFI, undated, p. 3)*	*To fulfil this vision and mission, SFI will focus on investments in the target areas that i. Develop Human Capital. . . . ii. Support Strong Ideas. . . . iii. Promote Partnerships. . . . In addition, SFI sets specific, time-based goals, e.g., between 2004 and 2008, SFI will [r]ecruit to Ireland at least 50 researchers or research teams whose accomplishments, potential and recognition by international peers place them amongst the top tier in their disciplines. (SFI, undated, p. 3)*
Bill and Melinda Gates Foundation	United States	Private	Building upon the unprecedented opportunities of the twenty-first century to improve equity in global health and learning (see Bill and Melinda Gates Foundation, undated[a]).	Bring innovations in health and learning to the global community (see Bill and Melinda Gates Foundation, undated[a]).
Carnegie Corporation of New York	United States	Private	*An organization that would "promote the advancement and diffusion of knowledge and understanding."* (Carnegie Corporation of New York, undated)	Support the development of a global community; use the enhanced availability of information to foster a sense of community worldwide (see Carnegie Corporation of New York, undated).
DARPA	United States	Public	Develop imaginative, innovative, and often high-risk research ideas offering a significant technological impact that will go beyond normal, evolutionary, developmental approaches and pursue these ideas from the demonstration of technical feasibility through the development of prototype systems (see DARPA, 2007).	Mines fundamental discoveries and accelerates their development and lowers their risks until they prove their promise and can be adopted (see DARPA, 2007).

Table A.1—Continued

Institution	Country	Public/ Private	Mission	Goals
NYSTAR	United States	Public	Encourage cooperative ventures between New York's institutions of higher education and not-for-profit institutions with private industry, including the removal of barriers that slow down or impede the development of university-industry partnerships (see NYSTAR, undated).	Increase the number of high-technology jobs and companies in New York through the commercialization of the research being conducted at the universities and research institutions throughout the state. Increase the total amount of federal and private research dollars being attracted to New York (see NYSTAR, undated).
BES	United States	Public	*Our mission is to deliver the remarkable discoveries and scientific tools that transform our understanding of energy and matter and advance the national, economic, and energy security of the United States. (BES, 2004, p. 10)*	*Advance the basic sciences for energy independence. . . . Harness the power of our living world. . . . Bring the power of the stars to earth. . . . Explore the fundamental interactions of energy, matter, time, and space. . . . Explore nuclear matter—from quarks to stars. . . . Deliver computing for the frontiers of science. . . . Provide the resource foundations that enable great science. (BES, 2004, pp. 12–13)*

NOTE: Where available, we present missions and goals as provided by the institution in its annual report, Web site, and other written documents. However, some institutions lack either a formal mission statement or an explicit list of goals, so labeled. In these cases, we offer proxies derived from the same sources.

strategic planning, approves new programs and major awards, and oversees the general operations of NSF. Board members—as many as two dozen, but usually less—include representatives from academia, government, and private industry with education and background in fields related to the priority research areas of the foundation. Usually most, if not all, have a Ph.D. or equivalent degree in a relevant subject area.

Some institutions make conscious decisions about board composition, in terms of the members' nationality, residency, and current professional ties. For example, FRST's board of directors includes only members with current ties to New Zealand–based organizations, and KACST's Supreme Committee consists entirely of government officials whose ministries are somehow invested in progress in science and technology plus three additional members of the prime minister's choosing. In some cases, the board includes representatives from particular professions or minority groups to address particular focus areas. For example, the board of directors of MSFHR, a health research funding organization in British Columbia, Canada, includes several representatives from health professions, and the board of FRST includes a native-population representative.

An institution executive, usually the top executive, and perhaps one or more independent advisory groups usually provide the information, advice, evaluations, and data the board needs to make its decisions. The director typically attends board meetings but does not always get a vote in the board's decisions or, as is the case with MSFHR, may vote only in the case of a tie. The board's decisions then inform the director of what needs to be implemented at the operational level. NSF, MSFHR, RWJF, and SFI all roughly conform to this structure.

NIH and the Bill and Melinda Gates Foundation both represent alternatives to the board-led, director-run governance model. In the case of NIH, the director takes on the principal leadership role in the absence of a governing board. The director is responsible for providing leadership to all of the individual institutes (program areas) from the perspective of the institution's overall mission, by gathering and synthesizing information and advice from staff, researchers, the external scientific community, related public organizations, the U.S. Congress, and other governmental bodies. However, the director also reports to a higher-ranking U.S. government official. At the Gates Foundation, the founders, cochairs, and an executive team make up the leadership of the institution.

Relationships between advisory groups and the board are much more variable. Here, again, MSFHR offers an interesting example, in that it includes both a research advisory council (RAC) and advisory bodies consisting of a peer-review committee and task forces. The RAC advises and makes recommendations on all research-related peer-review issues. The board appoints all members, although current RAC members may provide input. The chair of the RAC sits on the foundation board but does not vote. The advisory bodies, which the RAC appoints, conduct the actual merit review of proposals submitted to the foundation and subsequently make recommendations to the RAC. Members are chosen to represent both a variety of sectors of health research and a broad range of expertise.

Terms on both the RAC and the advisory bodies are two years, with the exception of the chair of the RAC, whose term is only one year. Members of the advisory bodies may renew their terms up to three times, for a maximum of a six-year term, with the exception of the chair, who may renew his or her term only twice. An effort is made to stagger the members' terms on the advisory bodies to ensure continuity.

FRST employs a similar model, with area-specific reference groups appointed to conduct the selection process and recommend action on proposals to the board. And the NSF structure includes extensive advisory boards made up of experts drawn from the external scientific community.

With the notable exceptions of NIH and the Gates Foundation, the institutions that we considered favor a board-led approach. Though some institutions, e.g., MSFHR, the Sloan Foundation, and FRST, give ultimate grant-making authority to their governing boards, micromanagement does not appear to be prevalent; rather, a model of active but typically broad-based engagement seems to dominate. On balance, we recommend this model for QNRF. While it would give the director significant authority to operate the organization, it would draw on a wide base of knowledge, experience, and interest to establish the overall direction of QNRF, set policy, and provide institutional oversight.

Award Processes and Funding Mechanisms

We address award processes and funding mechanisms in three parts: first, soliciting proposals; second, options for funding mechanisms; and third, reviewing proposals and making awards.

Soliciting Proposals. Award processes and funding mechanisms can be custom-designed to encourage projects that most closely align with the institution's mission and goals while ensuring that the institution is funding high-quality research and remaining flexible enough to allow for future growth. At the outset, the institution must determine what type of projects and research it would most like to fund. We observed two broad strategies: (1) consulting field experts, perhaps even the researchers who may be performing the research themselves, about the most pressing needs or promising directions in the field; and (2) formulating RFPs based on the goals and needs of the foundation.

To some extent, DARPA follows the first strategy. It encourages direct contact between program managers and potential grantees and welcomes unsolicited preproposals even if the proposed project does not fall within the currently funded research areas. Similarly, BES engages the federal laboratories in the process of determining what the RFPs will look like for that year. FRST also follows the consultation-based RFP model but casts the net even more widely, gathering advice and suggestions from many different groups of stakeholders including those from academia, industry, and government.

The second strategy is somewhat more common, as it can be narrowed or made very general, according to the needs of the institution. Following this strategy, the foundation or program formulates its RFPs relatively independently—though not necessarily in isolation—of stakeholders, based on considerations of its goals and the state of research in the field.[2] One of the duties of the RAC at MSFHR is to recommend content for RFPs to the governing board. NSF and NIH formulate somewhat more general RFPs for funding external research in this way. This strategy is particularly useful when an institution's goals are less discipline-oriented, such as those that focus on education or training grants. REU, for example, formulates RFPs to emphasize program elements specific to the active participation of undergraduates in research, while keeping the subject area in which they conduct that research general enough to allow innovation.

We recommend a combination of the two approaches for QNRF: consulting with experts in the field to help identify specific needs in particular research areas and formulating RFPs internally to help ensure fulfillment of the fund's mission and goals. With regard to undergraduate research, the REU approach offers considerable appeal in its generality.

Choosing Among Funding Mechanisms. Institutions can choose from a wide range of funding mechanisms to achieve their goals. Whether a grant will support a single project (e.g., an individual researcher, a group of researchers, students) or a cluster of related projects (e.g., the development of an entire research program or center, student research program, public-private partnership) may determine the level and flexibility of funding or the length of guaranteed continuous funding or even the level to which potential grantees are involved in the solicitation and project design process. Indeed, DARPA's model requires very flexible funding schemes, whereas REU awards only two types of grants—those supplementing existing grants to support the addition of undergraduate researchers and those used for setting up new sites for programs dedicated to creating research opportunities for undergraduates.

Falling somewhere in the middle, and potentially most useful to QNRF, SFI maintains a list of clearly defined and structured funding mechanisms, which allows for simplified and standardized solicitation and selection processes. The list provides tools for funding several different kinds of projects, each of which addresses one or more of the foundation's goals. The mechanisms include individual scientist awards, campus-industry partnership grants, visiting researcher awards, and workshop and conference grants. Most, if not all, of these mechanisms seemed potentially relevant to QNRF.

The Alfred P. Sloan Foundation presents another midrange option. It uses what it calls officer grants to allow some flexibility within an otherwise standardized funding scheme (i.e., competitive fellowships, direct support of research, center development, and directed support). A program officer can choose to award the grant at any time, thereby enabling the foundation to respond quickly outside the usual process cycle—the foundation can take advantage of special funding opportunities as they arise. Similarly, the Carnegie Corporation offers another

---

[2] Although the institution may not appear to go outside of itself for consultative purposes, its stakeholders may be well represented on its boards or advisory committees.

alternative through what it calls discretionary grants. These are grants of less than $25,000 that are made upon the approval of the president and then reported to the board.

Reviewing Proposals and Making Awards. Regarding award processes, peer review is the most common approach among the institutions that we reviewed. The NSF and NIH models are particularly well known and well respected, having longstanding histories of generating high-quality research. For NSF review panels, members are chosen by program officers and are charged with assessing the quality of a proposal based on two general criteria: the intellectual merit and the broader effects of the proposed activity. These review panels then recommend a funding action for each proposal. NIH follows a similar two-step approach: first, expert scientific review panels, composed of highly regarded non-NIH scientists, review the proposals; second, independent advisory councils, including members of the public, review them to help ensure that NIH receives advice from a cross-section of the U.S. population in its deliberations. NIH considers recommendations from both sets of reviews when deciding funding actions.

An alternative to peer review is to rely on reviews conducted by personnel within the foundation. The Sloan Foundation uses this model, as does DARPA, to some extent, placing less emphasis on peer review to support particularly innovative ideas.

For QNRF, it would be especially important to tie funding decisions to a peer review process, to establish itself as a credible research institution internationally. Both NSF and NIH offer good basic frameworks for peer review. Peer review, when combined with a solicitation process and funding mechanisms that emphasize QNRF's strategic goals, while allowing for the flexibility to take advantage of the opportunities and needs among the community of potential grant recipients, would help QNRF credibly address all aspects of its mission.

Monitoring and Evaluation Processes

Foundations and programs undertake monitoring and evaluation on at least two levels: the foundation or program level and the project level.[3] Monitoring and evaluation at the foundation or program level tends to consider the totality of an institution's activities over a variety of functional areas. For this reason, we refer to it as *institutional monitoring and evaluation*. NIH, for example, organizes the performance goals for its research into five functional areas: (1) scientific research outcomes, (2) communication and transfer of results, (3) capacity building and research resources, (4) strategic management of human capital, and (5) program oversight and improvement. Whereas project-level monitoring and evaluation tends to consider the achievements of particular awards or endeavors, project-level assessments may also provide inputs to broader institutional assessments; that is, a foundation or program may look at project-level indicators, such as the number of publications or patents, to assess its overall performance in a particular area, such as research outcomes or communication.

Government-sponsored institutions tend to have comparatively well developed and articulated monitoring and evaluation processes, at both the institutional and project levels.[4] Private foundations tend to require some form of reporting, either at the institutional or project level, but they generally provide less detailed information about their practices.

Conducting Institutional-Level Evaluation. At the institutional level, NIH has developed a set of objective or quantitative performance goals and descriptive achievement criteria, which

---

[3]   Evaluation also occurs at intermediate levels, e.g., by assessing the performance of clusters of projects or portfolios.

[4]   For U.S. government programs, these processes are a legal and administrative imperative.

it assesses through a combination of verifiable performance measures and independent external review.[5] In New Zealand, FRST has formulated a series of RS&T goals, which it has linked to measurable milestones and outcomes. Its evaluation process is a mixed-method approach, assessing outcome indicators, case studies, user surveys, stakeholder surveys, intellectual property performance, bibliometric studies, and other work. SFI also has a set of strategic goals with corresponding metrics.

Among the private foundations, we found less information. A 2004 RWJF case study indicated the development and adoption of comprehensive evaluation methods, including an "impact framework," "scorecard," and third-party appraisals, but RWJF is a pioneer in the field (see Guidice and Bolduc, 2004). The most common form of institutional evaluation appears to be the annual report, which includes a balance sheet and income statement. Under most circumstances, these reports are legally required in the United States. Some foundations may allow opportunities for their governing boards and advisory council to conduct self-evaluation or provide evaluative inputs. For example, MSFHR describes the evaluation protocol for its research advisory council:[6]

> Annually, the Council will review its goals and objectives, performance and Terms of Reference and report to the Board on this review. The report will include any resulting recommendations for changes to the Terms of Reference, as well as advice on Foundation Peer Review activities and processes. (MSFHR, 2001)

For more on recent trends in institutional performance measurement in the not-for-profit sector, see the discussion under "Reports on Foundation Effectiveness," later in this appendix.

As we discuss in the section on planning and growth, institutional-level evaluation is crucial to QNRF, even in its early phases. An in-depth comprehensive evaluation of the fund's performance in meeting its goals and furthering its mission is important not only for planning for growth, but also for solidifying QNRF's role in the research community in Qatar and maximizing its impact on research worldwide. To promote transparency and better serve Qatar, we also recommended formally incorporating outside views, through surveys or external reviews.

Monitoring Projects. At the project level, NIH requires that grantees submit annual and final progress reports, with detailed descriptions of accomplishments. A standardized form for annual reporting calls for information on grant-derived publications and other project-generated resources, including "data, research materials . . ., protocols, software or other information available to be shared with other investigators" (HHS, 2006, p. 16). In addition to a standard annual progress report, REU explicitly requires that all projects for undergraduate research participation design and implement a project evaluation plan. REU allows "much latitude" in the plan's design, referencing an online handbook for project evaluation and offering the following general guidance:

> Evaluation may involve periodic measures throughout the project to ensure that it is progressing satisfactorily according to the project plan, and may involve pre-project and post-project measures aimed at determining the degree of student learning that has been achieved as a result of the project. Additionally, it is highly desirable to have a structured

---

[5] External review has become increasingly prominent in U.S. agency evaluations. For all but its management goals, NSF relies entirely on qualitative reviews undertaken by external bodies.

[6] MSFHR is funded by, but operates at arms' length from, the government of British Columbia.

means of tracking participating students beyond graduation with the aim of gauging the degree to which the REU Site experience has been a lasting influence as they follow their career paths. (NSF, undated, p. 7)

Among the private foundations, current practices range from rigorous reporting requirements with significant financial controls to near–laissez faire. As an example of rigor, RWJF calls for a combination of financial, narrative, and bibliographic reporting. Regarding financial controls, it requires that grantees gain approval for spending in any budgetary category that exceeds 5 percent of the initial projection—even if overall spending is within the budget. For the narrative and bibliographic reports, RWJF provides a 27-page instruction book, with exhaustive details on requirement for content and format. The Sloan Foundation allows more flexibility in connection with annual and final reporting but may ask some grantees "to develop and continually update a web-site concerning the project" (Alfred P. Sloan Foundation, undated [a]).

Project-level monitoring and evaluation are necessary for building a base of consistent, high-quality, and well-documented research support. However, QNRF's mission requires flexibility in project design and methods of funding to accommodate potentially unique national needs. For these reasons, reporting requirements may require some tailoring to circumstances in different program areas; that is, a research grant, an undergraduate research and education award, and a conference or workshop should have somewhat different reporting requirements.

Nevertheless, certain basic requirements should cut across most if not all program areas. For example, all award recipients on multiyear funding should submit progress reports annually and final progress reports within a short period of project completion, e.g., 90 days. Reports should clearly identify project accomplishments in specific dimensions, such as those set out in NIH guidance for grant reports, and provide an accurate accounting of the use of funds. QNRF will need this detailed information to assess its performance at a higher, intuitional level.

Approaches to Institutional Planning and Growth

Several of the selected institutions draw on internal evaluation processes and community perceptions to guide planning. Functional priorities also feature prominently. These approaches can be mutually reinforcing. In broad terms, successful institutional expansion requires a clear plan of action, addressing growth in either the depth or breadth of programs and demonstrating alignment with recognized needs.

Drawing on Evaluation Processes. Several institutions consider the results of regular evaluation processes in planning for future operations and growth. A particularly salient example of this is in the way in which RWJF has approached the issue of planning through recent changes to its annual self-evaluation process. Individual program-area teams were asked to articulate their program strategies and goals and to design some measures of progress. In some cases, teams created a vision of what success would look like in five to 10 years, identified areas in which foundation support could lead to "great change," and developed a logic model that would plausibly accomplish the intended change. In this way, they were able to create for themselves a clear guide for future growth in their program area.

BES requires similar planning from its own national laboratories, which receive the majority of its funding every year. Though funded annually, each lab must develop an institutional plan for the subsequent three to five years, in which it articulates the intended direction of growth, including projected research priorities, for each of its programs. FRST similarly conducts somewhat regular evaluations and revisions of its highly detailed research portfolio (focus area) descriptions, through which it aims to ensure the best overall contribution of research to New Zealand's national needs. It also includes a process for planning and prioritizing the desired direction of funded projects in that area over the subsequent three years.

In each case, the staff most closely associated with a program area is responsible for planning in its particular field of research, through a process that stems from information gained through careful self-evaluation.

Responding to Community Perceptions. Some institutions weigh community perceptions heavily in their planning processes. They may look to stakeholders for insight as to whether they are meeting expectations or missing opportunities. In effect, they ask stakeholders, "How are we doing?"

For example, RWJF surveys staff, applicants, grantees, policymakers, field experts, and the general public to determine how stakeholders view the foundation and its degree of influence. On the basis of this input, it designs strategies and plans that work from its current state toward the foundation's overall goals. Similarly, SFI, a recently established grant-making institution, plans to engage the community regularly to identify promising new areas in support of its mission; "SFI will build and strengthen scientific and engineering research and its infrastructure in the areas of greatest strategic value to Ireland's long-term competitiveness and development" (SFI, undated, p. 3). Initially, SFI will focus on fields that underpin biotechnology and information and communication technology, noting that Ireland's affiliation with leading industries in related fields gives it strategic advantages in these areas (SFI, undated). DARPA, drawing heavily on external perspectives, relies on direct interaction and input from researchers in the field to determine future opportunities and investment paths.

Focusing on Functional Priorities. In formulating plans, some institutions have chosen to focus on functional priorities, such as collaborative endeavors or educational programs, in determining who or what they will fund now and in the near future. Particular aspects of the way such foundations set their priorities and plan for future organizational growth may be useful models for QNRF. For example, NYSTAR has chosen to focus on the translation of high-technology investment into economic development for the state of New York. To do this, it is prioritizing funding to centers devoted to initiating and supporting public-private partnerships in applied science research endeavors.

As another example, REU is geared toward creating and maintaining diverse and worthwhile research opportunities for undergraduates. It has designed specialized proposal-review criteria and funding mechanisms to ensure that this priority is met. Specifically, it provides funds to institutions interested in creating programs on their home campuses for undergraduates interested in getting involved in research and to researchers willing to devote some time and money to designing a meaningful and worthwhile role for one or more undergraduate researchers in their ongoing projects. UROP shares a similar mission with REU but uses a different funding strategy. Here, the funding is awarded to individual students who have proposed to do research with faculty or other research staff at one of the participating institutions, namely MIT or Wellesley College.

QNRF has to make an effort to include aspects of each of these approaches to institutional planning and growth. At the outset, it required a keen awareness of its role in Qatar. Soliciting views from those affected by QNRF activities will be crucial to determining when and how the fund should expand. In this regard, the SFI, RWJF, and DARPA approaches to community engagement should guide QNRF. However, QNRF should not limit itself to this approach. It should also develop regular processes of self-evaluation, like RWJF has, as they will provide necessary information to fine tune—and occasionally substantially modify—the QNRF growth strategy.

Reports on Foundation Effectiveness

Our review of recent reports on foundation effectiveness, sponsored by CEP, the World Economic Forum (WEF), and others, suggests that certain approaches to management, cutting across a range of private foundations, tend to convey effectiveness almost irrespective of the foundation's defining characteristics. Here, we present findings in two related areas: governance, particularly the role of the board, and assessment methods.

Governance and the Role of the Board

The collection of reports strongly suggests the importance of active board engagement. Most recently, CEP published the results of a survey of the CEOs of the 250 largest U.S. foundations. The survey, which was intended to gather information about the governance practices of foundation boards, found that "five key variables are strong predictors of the degree to which a CEO considers his or her board effective. . . . In order of significance, they are:

- Involvement in assessing the foundation's overall performance;
- Bringing thought-provoking and important concerns to the attention of the CEO;
- Responding to recent media and legislative scrutiny through board-level discussions of governance;
- A lower proportion of donor's family members serving on the board; and
- Actively representing the foundation to the public" (Buchanan, 2004, p. 2).

Further elaborating on the principle of active engagement, the surveyed CEOs saw the most effective boards as "meeting more frequently and spending more time on foundation business outside of scheduled board meetings" and "substantially more involved in assessing the foundation's social impact, contributing subject-specific expertise, and developing the foundation's strategy" (Buchanan, 2004, p. 3). The report concluded, "Boards that are perceived as most effective by their CEOs are highly proactive and deeply engaged in guiding and evaluating the substantive work of the foundation" (Buchanan, 2004, p. 3).

However, the call for active engagement is not a call for micromanagement. The CEP report notes that "the data . . . seem to reflect a broader shift in the expectations of board governance from addressing basic 'operational' aspects, such as approving grant dockets or reviewing investments, toward the more substantive issues of policy, strategy, and social impact" (Buchanan, 2004, p. 13).

Relating to the next topic, assessment methods, CEP once described the board as "the ultimate audience for performance measures and the one body to which foundation management is explicitly and formally accountable" (CEP, 2002b, p. 36). On that basis, it found three areas in which boards contribute to effectiveness: accountability, financial and strategic stewardship, and active engagement. However, a roughly contemporaneous CEP seminar report described three challenges that boards faced in fulfilling their oversight roles: (1) a culture of "gentility and politeness, which too often engender a reluctance to engage in healthy criticism, admissions of failure, and candid learning"; (2) a lack of "role clarity"; and (3) a lack of mechanisms for board self-assessment, to provide and receive feedback on their own performance (Boston Foundation, 2002, p. 5).

A report prepared by the Nonprofit Sector Strategy Group of the Aspen Institute addresses governance more broadly, placing the issue of board engagement in the larger frame of key findings on foundation accountability and effectiveness (Aspen Institute, 2002). With regard to accountability, the report called for increased transparency; enhanced public access through board membership, advisory councils, and external review; strengthened foundation staff and board engagement and preparation; and strengthened regulatory oversight. The report also linked foundation effectiveness to board engagement, suggesting that effectiveness is likely to suffer without it (Aspen Institute, 2002, pp. 4–11).

Assessment Methods

Some recent reports have considered options and best practices in assessment for private foundations, focusing on what we previously termed the *institutional level*. Though none indicates the appropriateness of a universal approach, each suggests the importance of some basic considerations, relating to results, strategy, and administration.

In *Philanthropy Measures Up*, Global Leaders for Tomorrow (GLT) provides an overview of approaches to measuring philanthropic impact, based on a review of 18 institutions' and four consulting firms' practices, finding that most of the organizations follow a "traditional results measurement framework" that links inputs to activities, activities to outputs, and outputs to outcomes (GLT, 2003, p. 4). It refers to this as the *results approach*. Unfortunately, some of the report's most effective examples of the results approach appear to be among the most institution-specific, i.e., nontransferable, and costly. GLT also makes reference to two additional approaches: performance and comparative. As it defines them, "Performance approaches monitor grantee or foundation/donor/corporate performance versus pre-set operational, financial, and programmatic goals, while Comparative approaches can monitor grantee and philanthropist performance versus their peers (also known as benchmarking)" (GLT, 2003, p. 4). A series of organizational profiles indicates that some organizations use elements of all three approaches, in combination.

Drawing from the profiles, GLT also presents a summary of best practices for measuring impact. Not every cited practice is relevant to the proposed QNRF, but many are. We provide bracketed notes for some of the practices, in an effort to clarify or reinterpret them for QNRF.

- "Participatory evaluation [including grantees] is critical;
- "Align the strategies for constructive change of an organization [align QNRF's desired outcomes and its mission] with concrete goals and systems to support the measurement of progress towards those goals;
- "Develop a selection [award] process that funds organizations [researchers] you can *trust* have meaningful missions [appropriate research objective];
- "Don't let measurement prevent innovation and risk taking;
- "Evaluation should be a learning tool. . . ;

- "Explore using commonly accepted measures of success from the field as your measures for success [look to other research foundations and programs for examples];
- "Developing and supporting the implementation of transparent, easy to understand measurements provides a means for donors to help . . . grantees bring in new funding [developing a transparent measurement system that can demonstrate results may help QNRF to attract funding partners and collaborators];
- "Fully fund evaluation on both ends [both the grant maker and grantee];
- "Know your audience, and pick a measurement approach to meet [its] needs; and
- "Know exactly what you want to measure—you can't measure it all" (GLT, 2003, p. 5).

Expanding on the concept of evaluation as a learning tool, GLT (2003, p. 65) warns of "the possibility of superficial measurements driving NGO's towards superficial impacts." As the most important thing—i.e., effects—may be the most difficult to measure, institutions may have an unfortunate tendency to focus on those things that are most readily measured but least important. In so doing, evaluation may lead institutions away from their mission and goals.

Predating GLT effort, CEP conducted in-depth interviews with 18 CEOs of private foundations in the United States, seeking answers to two basic questions: What does it mean for a foundation to perform well, and how can performance be measured? Despite differences in vocabularies and emphases across respondents, CEP found that CEOs tend to judge their foundations' performance in three interrelated areas, ranked by priority.

- "Achieving impact: Making progress toward the foundation's goals and delivering results.
- "Setting the agenda: Defining the foundation's fields of interest, specific goals, and overall approach to its work.
- "Managing operations: Monitoring internal processes and managing the foundation's human and financial resources" (CEP, 2002a, p. 3).

However, CEP also notes that the first category is both the most important and the most difficult to measure. As a consequence, CEOs tend to use agenda-setting and management measures to get at impact, "accepting that a well-managed organization with clear goals is likely to achieve greater impact" (CEP, 2002a, p. 3). Like GLT, CEP offers a warning that measures "might become 'blunt instruments' that would distort foundation behavior and decision making" (CEP, 2002a, p. 4).

The aforementioned RWJF case study on performance assessment demonstrates how the pieces fit together in a real-world setting (see Guidice and Bolduc, 2004). RWJF uses a balanced-scorecard methodology that measures accomplishments in four areas: impact, program, service to grantees and customers, and staff. It has also adopted an impact framework that groups grants into portfolios related to particular strategies. On this basis, RWJF can measure its strategic progress through the totality of its related efforts. The approach is predicated on a simple logic model that links grants to outputs, outputs to outcomes, and outcomes, ultimately, to impacts on health and health care.

In recounting the history of the RWJF experience with performance assessment, the case study derives five lessons learned for initiating performance measurement: (1) the perfect time to begin will never exist and consensus will never be reached—strong leadership from the senior staff and board are crucial to getting the process off the ground, (2) practicality is critical, (3) reinforcement of a learning culture is important, (4) staff need help in setting goals, and (5) an end point must be articulated (Guidice and Bolduc, 2004, p. 8).

The evidence on performance-assessment methods suggests the importance of developing measures of impacts while recognizing the importance of strategic planning and operational considerations in generating results—and avoiding the pitfalls of superficiality. A full assessment may require a combination of measures, touching on all three areas. And, benchmarking may be necessary. Moreover, the high level of effort required to develop these measures in the context of an overall assessment system suggests the importance of developing both the measures and the system as soon as possible in the life of an institution, with the intent to iterate and adjust them over time.

Conclusions and Recommendations

We reviewed several foundations, programs, and recent reports to improve our understanding of the ways in which research-based institutions develop and implement organizational structures and governance principles, award processes and funding mechanisms, monitoring and evaluation processes, and approaches to institutional planning and growth. On this basis, we provided recommendations for QNRF.

Organizational Structures and Governance Principles

We recommend a board-led approach, similar to that of NSF and several other foundations and programs. While it would give the director significant authority to operate the organization, it would draw on a wide base of knowledge, experience, and interest to establish the overall direction of QNRF, set policy, and provide institutional oversight. In addition, QNRF should consider forming one or more advisory committees to provide both expertise and additional links to stakeholders.

Per both the foundation and program reviews and the recent CEP reports, we also recommend an actively engaged board, i.e., one that participates in institutional assessments, brings "thought-provoking and important concerns" to the director's attention, provides "financial and strategic stewardship," and periodically and candidly assesses its own performance. We also discourage micromanagement.

Award Processes and Funding Mechanisms

We provide recommendations for soliciting proposals, choosing among funding mechanisms, and reviewing proposals and making awards.

With regard to solicitation, we recommend a combination of two general approaches: (1) consulting with experts in the field to help identify specific needs in particular research areas and (2) formulating RFPs internally, within QNRF, to help ensure fulfillment of the fund's overarching mission and goals. With regard to undergraduate research, the REU approach, which requires program elements that are specific to the active participation of undergraduate researchers but does not prescribe particular research areas, offers considerable appeal in its generality.

With regard to funding mechanisms, we recommend an SFI-like list of clearly defined and structured funding mechanisms, to allow for simplified and standardized solicitation and selection processes. The list would provide tools for funding different kinds of projects, such as research grants, undergraduate research-based education awards, and workshop and conference grants, each of which would address one or more of the fund's goals.

Regarding selections and award making, we recommend peer review. Tying funding decisions to a peer-review process can help to establish the fund as a credible research institution, internationally. Both NSF and NIH offer good basic frameworks. Peer review, when combined with a solicitation process and funding mechanisms that emphasize QNRF's strategic goals, will help QNRF credibly address all aspects of its mission.

Monitoring and Evaluation Processes

We provide recommendations for both institutional- and project-level evaluations and monitoring.

Institutional-level evaluation is crucial, even in the earliest phases of QNRF. A rigorous evaluation of the fund's performance in meeting its goals and furthering its mission is important not only for planning future growth, as addressed below, but also for solidifying its role in the research community in Qatar and maximizing its impact on research worldwide. To promote transparency and better serve Qatar, we also recommend formally incorporating outside views, through surveys or third-party reviews.

Project-level monitoring and evaluation are necessary for building a base of consistent, high-quality, and well-documented research support. However, if QNRF supports several funding mechanisms, it may need to tailor its reporting requirements; that is, a research grant, an undergraduate research-based education award, and a workshop or conference grant should have somewhat different reporting requirements. Nevertheless, certain basic requirements should cut across most, if not all, program areas. For example, all award recipients should submit annual and final progress reports on a timely basis. The reports should clearly identify project accomplishments in specific dimensions, such as publications, reports, and patents. They should also provide an accurate accounting of the use of funds. QNRF will need this detailed information to assess its performance at a higher, institutional level.

Per CEP, RWJF, and other recent reports, the evidence on performance-assessment methods suggests the importance of developing measures of institutional- and project-level effects while recognizing the importance of planning processes and operational considerations in generating results. A full, multilevel assessment may require a combination of measures, touching on all three areas—effects, planning, and operations. Moreover, given the amount of effort needed, the evidence also suggests the importance of developing both the measures and an overall assessment system as soon as possible in the life of an institution, with the intent to iterate and adjust practices over time.

Approaches to Planning and Growth

Several of the selected institutions look to internal evaluation processes, community perceptions, and functional priorities to guide planning. Soliciting views from those affected by QNRF activities will be crucial to determining when and how the fund should expand. In this regard, the SFI, RWJF, and DARPA approaches to community engagement, in which they look to stakeholders for guidance, provide appropriate models. However, QNRF should also develop regular processes of self-evaluation, such as that used by RWJF, as they will provide the necessary information to fine tune—and occasionally substantially modify—the QNRF growth strategy.

Overall, successful expansion will require a clear plan of action, addressing growth in either the depth or breadth of programs and demonstrating alignment with recognized needs.

In conclusion, we note that the call for outside views features prominently in virtually every dimension of institutional planning and operations, ranging from governance to growth. Perhaps one of the most effective ways in which the fund can remain true to its mission and goals is by actively seeking outside views as soon and regularly as practicable.

Managing Intellectual Property Rights

Eric Talley

A prospective by-product of QNRF's mission is a steady flow of inventions and creative works, many of which are likely to have appreciable market potential. Preparing for this prospect has some urgency. The IPR regime will directly influence the behavior and receptivity of the possible participants in the QNRF program. It is therefore imperative that the design of QNRF accord significant attention to the allocation of downstream IPRs. This appendix undertakes a comparative review of various models of technology transfer, both as used in other nations and as applied to the underlying goals of QNRF.

Before commencing with our review, we note that IPRs are necessarily a broad subject and, as such, are usually subdivided into three constituent domains: (1) patents, which cover the protection of *novel and useful inventions and ideas*; (2) copyrights, which protect not ideas, but rather the *unique expression* of ideas; and (3) trademarks, which cover unique means for *identifying the source* of a good or service. Because the chief enterprise of QNRF is to fund research, it is unlikely that trademark concerns will play an appreciable role in the design of the program. Copyright concerns may well come to play a role in the medium to long term, as QNRF begins to broaden its focus into the arts and humanities. However, given that the initial phases of QNRF are likely to focus on scientific research (where patent concerns are predominant), and given that patents are the area in which the stakes (to date) are the largest, we tailored our analysis accordingly: to focus on patent rights.

Overview of Options

To motivate the discussion, it is helpful to consider the underlying economic stakes for IPRs among universities and other public research organizations (PROs).[1] The past two decades have seen an era of tremendous patenting activity across all quarters of the research community. However, the trend is probably the most acute at research universities, who are recipients of most government-funded research. For example, in the United States, as shown in Figure B.1, the number of total U.S. patents granted has increased at an annual rate of approximately 6.9 percent since 1950 and at around 11 percent since 1980. While this large shift over the past quarter-century has been dramatic in its own right, the growth in patenting activities among research universities has eclipsed it by a significant margin. Indeed, while U.S. universities accounted for less than 0.2 percent of patents granted, they now are responsible for

---

[1] This category includes private companies, policy think tanks, and government research laboratories.

Figure B.1
Trends in U.S. Patents from 1960 to 1999

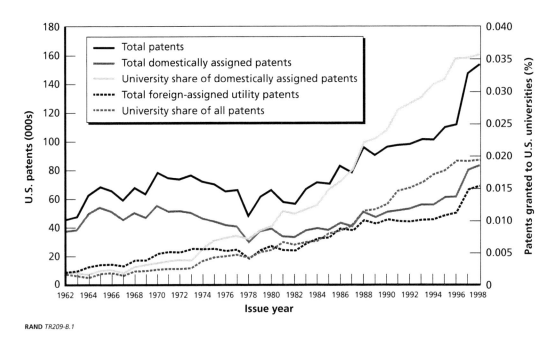

approximately 2.0 percent of all U.S. patents granted and more than 3.0 percent of patents granted to domestic recipients.

Not only has the sheer number of patents awarded to universities increased in both absolute and relative terms, but so too have the stakes involved in securing and exploiting those entitlements. A recent survey of 82 U.S. universities, for example, demonstrates that gross licensing revenues per institution more than doubled during the decade of the 1990s, from just under $1.9 million to just over $3.8 million (in constant 1996 dollars) (Mowery et al., 2001). This growth in revenue substantially exceeds the growth rate in university spending over the same course of time. And, while universities outside the United States are still somewhat behind, they are beginning to close the gap. In short, the IPR dimension of funded research is sophisticated. It is international. And it is big business.

Although QNRF need not mimic the institutional designs of governmental research funds in other nations, it is critical that the characteristics of that landscape be well understood for QNRF to situate its own intellectual property (IP) allocation system in a strategically viable position. It is therefore worthwhile to explore briefly whether—and to what extent—the structural characteristics of the IPR regime in other countries has contributed to the aforementioned trend.

Background and Legal Setting

Why have we witnessed a virtual explosion of patenting activities among research universities relative to other parties and institutions? The answer to this question is a complex one (and indeed has spawned a spirited debate in law and public policy literature). Part of the reason appears to be rooted in the simple pace of technological advancement in the late 1970s, which saw advances in biomedical research that began to portend commercial applications. Moreover, a number of important judicial opinions beginning in the 1980s expanded the scope of patentable innovations in a way that profoundly advantaged university research laboratories.[2] While these events were undoubtedly important, another critical piece in this puzzle was a discernable change in the very fabric of governmental policy regarding IPRs over inventions that come from publicly funded research (or PFR).

Formal policies regarding private patenting of innovations emerging from PFR were historically quite simple. For the most part, there were none—it was common policy within virtually all states that employed a national research funding mechanism that the output of PFR either belonged to the government or was in the public domain. In some exceptional cases (in which, for example, the recipient's efforts were largely a product of self-funded research), recipient entities or individual researchers were granted limited patent rights over their inventions. Even these exceptional instances, however, were largely governed by a loose patchwork of ad hoc decisions—frequently consisting of "deals" cut between the funding entity and the recipient.

Over the past quarter-century, however, it has been increasingly common for governments (particularly in developed states) to adopt formal policies regarding IPRs in funded research. Of those that have adopted such policies, a discernable trend appears to be in the direction of granting institutional-funding recipients the option to seek commercialization rights over the product of their funded research. The genesis of this trend is widely thought to have occurred in the United States, with the passage of the Bayh-Dole Act (BDA) (P.L. 96-517) (and the associated Stevenson-Wylder Technology Innovation Act [P.L. 96-480]), passed with the legislative goal of promoting the widespread use of federally sponsored inventions. The BDA essentially inverted the status quo default rule, granting funding recipients a presumptive right to seek patents for the products of their own research. Significantly, the legislation makes no distinction between application research (which leads immediately to discrete, marketable inventions) and basic research (which may lead to no immediate marketable inventions but provides the basic knowledge necessary to launch subsequent application-oriented research).

There are, however, two explicit exceptions in the BDA that would cause ownership to stay with (or revert back to) the funding entity or government. Under the first, the funding entity has "march in" rights—allowing it to take reversionary title to the invention when the funding recipient has made inadequate disclosures about it or has failed to exercise diligence in exploiting the invention. This exception has apparently never been employed in practice, perhaps testament to the appeal right that recipients enjoy, in which the evidentiary burden for demonstrating the predicate facts for march-in rights lies with the government (Rai and Eisenberg, 2003).

The second basic exception is that the BDA allows for the funding agreement to prohibit a recipient from procuring patent rights for reasons having to do with public policy (35 U.S.C. 202[a][i]). One presumptive public-policy rationale is the patent being inconsistent with the overarching goals of the statute. A second, and related, rationale, however, is the contractor not being located in the United States, not having a place of business located in the

---
[2]   See, e.g., *Diamond v. Chakrabarty* (1980) (permitting the patentability of a genetically engineered mouse).

United States, or not being subject to the control of a foreign government. We will return to these restrictions later.

Although, as noted above, the trend toward institutional entitlement to IPRs from funded research is thought to have started in the United States, a significant number of governments that maintain developed, funded research programs has embraced the core tenets of the BDA model. Table B.1 reports the default legal regime in 24 countries as of 2003. For both university and nonuniversity PRO research recipients, Table B.1 compares how the competing legal regimes assign IPRs among individual researchers, their research institutions, and the government.[3] Table B.1 also states (for countries from which this information was available) whether the recipient of the entitlement is under either a disclosure requirement or an exploitation duty (or both) as a condition for maintaining title. Regardless of who receives the ultimate assignment of IPRs, our research reveals that it is relatively common for the nonrecipient to receive a nonexclusive, nontransferable right to use IP for its own purposes.

From Table B.1, it appears clear that some countries have embraced a system that is largely similar to BDA provisions (and, in some cases, even more favorable to recipients). These include Australia, Austria, Belgium, Germany, Korea, Spain, and the United Kingdom. In contrast, there are notable exceptions. In Italy, for example, a 2001 statute formally granted rights to individual inventors over their institutions. Japan perhaps maintains the most dissimilar program to the BDA model, granting IPRs to either the individual researcher in a university or the government, depending on a decision made by a university-government committee. Moreover, Japan does not require either disclosure or exploitation for the inventor to retain title. Ireland charts perhaps a middle course, following a BDA model but not encumbering title with disclosure or exploitation duties. Russia, perhaps unsurprisingly, has been in a state of political flux. Although Russia still maintains a policy of governmental ownership, in 2001, Russia's Federal Service for Intellectual Property, Patents, and Trademarks (Rospatent) drafted recommendations favoring only limited governmental ownership and favoring organizational ownership; the State Duma later adopted resolutions to introduce changes or amendments to Russian patent law that constrain the right of state ownership of IP resulting from PFR.

Although not included in Table B.1, Singapore is perhaps an interesting comparison case for Qatar. Upon gaining its independence, the Singaporean government fostered a significant network of governmentally operated enterprises. To date, these enterprises still comprise nearly 15 percent of the country's gross domestic product, and the Singaporean government (often through these enterprises) appears to exercise ownership over many PFR products. Nevertheless, the Singaporean government also appears to be moving toward more of a BDA type of framework. In 2002, the Economic Review Committee (ERC) Sub-Committee on Entrepreneurship and Internationalisation (EISC) issued a comprehensive report on how Singapore could encourage a culture of entrepreneurship among private and university researchers (EISC, 2002). Among the report's many broad-based recommendations, EISC specifically recommended that the government adopt a policy of allowing recipients of federal funding to retain IPRs and to consider adopting legislation similar to the BDA if appropriate.

---

[3]   Note that Table B.1 provides *default* rules: In most of these countries, a contract between the party vested with the right and another individual can alter the default legal rights given in the local statute. Table B.1 notes governmental ownership in the United States as "sometimes," reflecting the fact that there are specific provisions in the BDA allowing the grantor to exercise march-in rights or declare exceptions. As practiced, however, such activities appear rare.

Table B.1
Cross-Country Comparison of Default Intellectual Property Right Allocation for Recipients of Federal Funds

Nation	University Recipients			Nonuniversity Recipients			Disclosure Duties	Exploitation Duties
	Institution	Individual	Government	Institution	Individual	Goverment		
Australia	Yes	No	No	Yes	No	No		Yes
Austria	Yes	No	No	Yes	No	No	Yes	
Belgium	Yes	No	No	Yes	No	No	Yes	Yes
Canada	Yes	Yes	No	Yes	No	No	Yes	Yes
Denmark	Yes	No	No	Yes	No	No	Yes	Yes
Finland	Yes	Yes	No	Yes	No	No	.	
France	Yes	No	No	Yes	No	No		
Germany	Yes	No	No	Yes	No	No	Yes	Yes
Iceland	No	Yes	No	Yes	No	No		
Ireland	Yes	No	No	Yes	No	No	No	No
Italy	No	Yes	No	No	Yes	No		
Japan	No	Yes	Sometimes	Yes	No	No	No	No
Korea	Yes	No	No	Yes	No	No		Yes
Mexico	Yes	No	No	Yes	No	No		
Netherlands	Yes	No	No	Yes	No	No		
Norway	Yes	No	No	Yes	No	No		No
Poland	Yes	No	No	Yes	No	No		
Russia	No	No	Yes	No	No	Yes		
South Africa	Yes	No	No	Yes	No	No		No
Spain	Yes	No	No	Yes	No	No	Yes	
Sweden	No	Yes	No	Yes	No	No		
Switzerland	Yes	Sometimes	No	Yes	No	No		
UK	Yes	No	No	Yes	No	No	Yes	Yes
United States	Yes	Sometimes	Sometimes	Yes	Sometimes	No	Yes	Yes

SOURCE: OECD (2003). This table distinguishes between university recipients and nonuniversity PROs, including private firms, think tanks, and government laboratories. When available, it also reports whether the IPR regime imposes disclosure or exploitation duties on recipients.

The bottom line of this inquiry is to make two observations. First, there is some heterogeneity among various states' approaches to IP assignment in funded research, both across countries and across time. Second, at the same time, there has been a notable amount of convergence over the past two decades toward the BDA model. This convergence may reflect any number of factors, and it is important to remain mindful that the best program for a developed national research fund may not be the best one for one in its infancy.

Balancing of Interests

In light of the consistent heterogeneity and reshuffling of IP protection in countries with developed national research funds and the discernable recent convergence to the BDA model, it is important that QNRF set a clear policy in articulating an appropriate regime for procuring and protecting IPRs. Many of the prospective funding recipients are now practiced in the art of procuring IPRs and thus can be expected to take full advantage of the rights they are accorded.

The underlying policy choice in allocating IPRs is often particularly difficult because it turns on a multiplicity of trade-offs. As noted in the introduction, the overarching, long-term goal of QNRF is to improve the general welfare of the people of Qatar and the region. There are numerous constituent parts to this goal, and three in particular for the IP allocation decision are given in Figure B.2.

First, QNRF should aim to cultivate an internal, stable, long-term resource that produces both high-quality research and tangible benefits for Qataris. A key to accomplishing this goal, of course, is to build a self-sustaining momentum around the program, so that it is in a position to compete in the longer term.

There are at least two key subsidiary considerations at play in thinking about how the value of the resource squares with IP protection. Primarily, it is important that the knowledge and inventions that emerge from QNRF-funded research create long-term value for the

**Figure B.2
Three Intellectual Property Allocation Decision Components of the
Qatar National Research Fund's Goal**

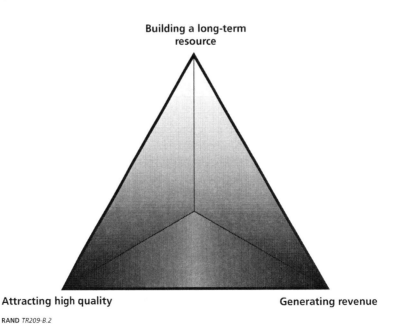

population and stakeholders of Qatar. It would be inconsistent with QNRF purposes for it to become a simple funding arm of research whose primary benefits flow immediately out of the system. Secondarily, it is important that the underlying legal protection of IPRs be gauged to encourage both primary and secondary research. IPRs that are too underprotective tend to discourage a significant amount of pioneering work, which provides the basis for subsequent discoveries. On the other hand, an IP policy that is overly protective may, ironically, retard research, as owners of pioneering patents use their privileged positions to hold up subsequent inventors for significant licensing fees, deterring their efforts in the process (see, e.g., Heller and Eisenberg, 1998).

Moving counterclockwise, a second important goal for QNRF is to be able to attract high-quality research *and research projects* in the short term. As noted, for QNRF to build momentum for the longer term, it needs to inculcate a sense of excitement and engagement from the onset. To do so, it will have to draw on and depend on the expertise of non-Qatari researchers. They must be motivated to locate in Qatar, move their labs, and possibly even export their other grant funds to the country. Here, QNRF must be cognizant about the fact that it will effectively be competing for those researchers and projects, who themselves may be able to choose among numerous potential locations. Their decisions may turn, at least in part, on the degree to which their subsequent IPRs are likely to be encumbered by governmental claims of ownership. While it is certainly plausible that many academic researchers are not heavily motivated by such considerations, the ultimate decisionmakers may actually be their home universities, who likely have some degree of leverage over them and frequently own an assignment of rights to all inventions the researcher creates. Therefore, it may be important for QNRF to allow for some degree of compatibility between Qatar's regime and those of other nations (by adopting compatible policies or least by allowing grantees to modify the default rule by mutual agreement).

Finally, while perhaps not the predominant goal of QNRF, it is important that the fund consider its prospects for generating revenue through licensing. Even when, as here, there are outside financial sources to provide funding, the fund's ability to expand over time may turn on locating additional sources of financial capital. In reality, IP licensing is unlikely to become an extraordinary source of revenue for QNRF, but, if it is to play any role, QNRF would necessarily have to consider retaining rights to at least some marketable inventions.

Options for the Qatar National Research Fund

With these underlying trade-offs in mind, we now proceed to identify a number of candidate "models" or templates that QNRF may wish to consider in crafting its own IPR allocation policy. While these models are far from exhaustive, we believe that each is at least a plausible candidate. Moreover, each navigates to a slightly different point in managing implicit policy concerns that we believe to be relevant.

Fund Ownership Model

Under this approach, either QNRF or the Qatar Foundation would retain title to all inventions that are produced, in substantial part, through funded research (what we shall refer to as *subject inventions*). At the same time, however, this allocation regime would constitute a "default" or background rule, so that QNRF and recipient could, in appropriate circumstances, negotiate an alteration in the underlying assignment.

This model's primary benefit is that it ensures that QNRF retains ultimate control over the innovations produced through its funding activities, and it will therefore always have a seat at the table in negotiating possible releases. Consequently, this approach is likely to minimize the danger that Qatari stakeholders (e.g., workers, citizens, customers, investors) will be disenfranchised from enjoying the benefits of commercially valuable QNRF-sponsored research projects. At the same time, however, this approach comes with some attendant costs. First, it paddles against the prevailing current in a number of countries (see analysis above), who are increasingly coming to adopt provisions resembling the Bayh-Dole approach (P.L. 96-517). At the very least, outsiders will have to account for the possibility that the underlying protective scheme in Qatar is different from those they encounter elsewhere. But in addition, such a system is likely to appear relatively unattractive to non-Qatari researchers (or their institutions), who are now used to receiving relatively undiluted IPRs from their inventions, in the short to medium term. Such a discontinuity may lead them to locate their most lucrative research programs outside of Qatar, which may undermine many QNRF goals. While case-by-case exceptions to the policy may mollify some of these concerns, they can also create significant ex ante uncertainty about downstream legal rights, which can itself dampen entrepreneurial efforts.

Joint Ownership Model

Under this approach, QNRF and the recipient would each own an undivided interest in the IPRs created by funded research, much like joint tenants who own undivided interests in a piece of real property. Licensing the invention would be subject to mutual agreement between the recipient and QNRF, effectively giving each party a veto right. As with the fund ownership model, under this approach, the grantee and QNRF would be free to negotiate alternative allocations when circumstances require.

The benefit of this approach is that it would continue to ensure that QNRF had an active voice in the use and exploitation of subject inventions, thereby contributing to the long-term resource potential of QNRF. It would also help to augment licensing revenue, at least on a pro rata basis with the recipient. The principal costs of this model, however, are potentially severe. First, such a scheme would put Qatar out of step with a cross-section of most countries (raising similar—if not more severe—concerns to those articulated above). Moreover, inherent in joint ownership is the absence of unilateral authority for one party or the other to make a decision about how to commercialize the invention without the other's consent, perhaps requiring difficult and protracted negotiations for each new exploitable technology. If such transaction costs are sufficiently severe, then the rate at which new technologies leave the research lab and penetrate the marketplace may be slowed significantly. Moreover, funding recipients may view their position as similar to that under the fund ownership model, in which QNRF retained IPRs, thereby diminishing their incentives to bring lucrative projects into Qatar.

Prevailing International Model

This approach would essentially replicate the default regime created by the Bayh-Dole model. Funding recipients (usually the institutions) would, by presumption, enjoy the option to patent their own inventions, an option that could only be extinguished ex ante in extraordinary cases involving national security or for strong public policy reasons. Under this model, the recipient would also be charged with a duty to disclose subject inventions fully to QNRF and a duty to exploit them in a fashion that ultimately benefits Qatari stakeholders. Should the grantee fail in either of these respects, QNRF would be entitled to march-in rights. Thus, for example, if a grantee procured IPRs from a subject invention but then used licensing revenues to expand its campus in Denmark, such a use would be inconsistent with its exploitation duties. On the other hand, if the grantee used licensing revenues to enhance its own infrastructure in Qatar (in the form of new buildings, labs, equipment, and the like), such activities would be consistent with exploitation in Qatar. Under this approach, a decision by QNRF to declare an exception or to utilize its march-in rights would be subject to an administrative appeal by the grantee, in which case QNRF would be required to demonstrate the basis for its decision. As with the fund ownership model, under this approach, the grantee and QNRF would be free to negotiate alternative allocations when circumstances require.

The primary benefits of this system are essentially the inverse of those of the fund ownership model, in that it removes a substantial amount of ownership uncertainty (as it has in the United States), and it borrows a familiar template for IP allocation that is now widespread. Moreover, by vesting presumptive rights in the recipients to procure a patent, the approach makes QNRF-funded research more attractive and provides an entrepreneurial incentive to bring other resources and personnel to Qatar. One potential cost of this approach is that, because the presumption of ownership lies with the recipient, it may prove costly for QNRF to assert its rights when it deems extraordinary circumstances to exist or to utilize march-in rights. (Recall, for example, that these rights are rarely if ever used by funding agencies in the United States.) This cost raises the possibility that Qatari stakeholders may lose out on at least some of the benefits of funded research, such as when an innovation is exploited in both Qatar and elsewhere. In addition, the strong policy of protection under the BDA may itself impose some costs as it begins to mature if the holders of mutually blocking patents are unable to reach consensual licensing agreements.

Canadian Model

Although it pursues a policy that implicitly favors patentability, Canada has adopted a model that might best be described as a modified version of the prevailing international approach but in which some of the default rights are subtly shifted toward the government. Although the government funding entity retains the right to claim IPRs over all subject inventions, a formal policy strongly encourages the funding entity to assign those rights to the recipient, except in enumerated exceptions (e.g., national security, express contract, or research intended principally to generate basic knowledge and information). QNRF would also possess march-in rights if the grantee failed to disclose its innovations or failed to exploit them in a fashion consistent with QNRF goals. The grantee may appeal the declaration of an exception or the use of march-in rights but would have to demonstrate that the QNRF decision was arbitrary, capricious, or an abuse of its discretion. As with the previous models, under this approach, the grantee and QNRF would be free to negotiate alternative allocations when circumstances require.

The essential difference between this approach and the BDA approach is that it increases the security that QNRF can expect should it decide that an enumerated exception exists or that grounds to exercise its march-in rights have been met: Indeed, under this approach, it is the recipient that must demonstrate that the funding entity's decision abused its discretion (rather than the other way around). At the same time, a strong policy statement favoring recipient patentability is one that is likely to provide recipients with some degree of confidence in the overall security of their IPRs, especially if it is accompanied by a track record in which QNRF utilizes its exemption authority conservatively and judiciously. To be sure, this approach runs the danger of increasing regulatory uncertainty relative to countries that follow the BDA model, but the burden here would be significantly smaller than in the fund ownership or joint ownership models. Moreover, the discontinuity between this policy and that of other countries would be smaller, and, in fact, Qatar would be selecting a template that is already used by at least one developed country.

Which Option to Choose?

This is obviously a difficult question to answer, since it entails not only an understanding of the trade-offs implicit with each model (outlined above), but it also requires a clear picture of how much weight each trade-off should receive. Ultimately, of course, this latter decision is a normative judgment for QNRF to make. However, we can offer at least a few guiding principles.

- Whichever policy QNRF adopts, it is important that the policy clearly articulate the underlying parameters of IPR allocation in a transparent manner. If, for example, QNRF opts for a regime allocating property rights to recipients with some exceptions, the factual predicates for those exceptions must be well known, easy to interpret, and made salient to recipients. Although the applicability of an exception will often be a judgment call (particularly in close cases), QNRF should carefully establish a consistent and predictable track record for invoking them.
- The framework should reflect the overarching goal of QNRF to benefit the people of Qatar and the region, not as a conduit for Qatari financing of research that is commercialized in a way that confers no benefit on the people (or other stakeholders of Qatar). Here, it is important to keep in mind the fact that there are multiple means for exploiting IPRs in a fashion consistent with QNRF goals, including the indirect benefits that would accrue were a grantee to direct licensing revenues from its own exploitation toward expenditures on infrastructure within Qatar.
- There are some potentially appreciable costs to being too far out of step with the regimes adopted in other countries. For better or worse, most nations with active federal funding programs for research appear to be converging on the BDA model. While a small deviation from the BDA regime would likely prove palatable to most stakeholders, a significant break from the status quo ante could prove costly to both the short- and long-term quality of QNRF-supported research.[4]
- QNRF must be mindful of the transaction costs that ownership structure can bring about. Notwithstanding the fact that the aforementioned models would constitute "default rules" subject to alteration by negotiated agreement, such negotiations are not costless. Each time an underlying ownership structure necessitates protracted bargaining between interested stakeholders, the rate of diffusion of technical innovations will likely slow and QNRF goals will likely be frustrated. Consequently, all else held constant, QNRF should avoid IPR ownership regimes that will likely depend routinely on bargaining around poor allocations or the exercise of mutual veto rights among interested stakeholders.

---

[4]   This competitive aspect of the design is sharpened by the fact that other countries in the region, such as the United Arab Emirates, have begun to court foreign universities aggressively.

Either the prevailing international or Canadian model would strike an acceptable balance for QNRF. The prevailing international model would vest slightly greater power in the hands of grantees than would the Canadian model. Further, the prevailing international model is likely better known and understood by grantees throughout the world. The Canadian model, however, would offer an administrative advantage to QNRF by making it easier for it to exercise its rights when clearly in the national interest. This option still captures the advantages of commonality with most other nations and substantially preserves the incentives to innovate offered by the prevailing international model. While Canada has chosen to implement its approach through an administrative policy framework, Qatar could incorporate similar provisions in law for use by QNRF and other funders. The ultimate choice between these two models should be based on further analysis of (1) Qatar's ability to attract distinguished researchers under a Canadian model that deviates, however slightly, from the prevailing international model and (2) the nature and extent of circumstances in which QNRF would seek to exercise its rights. If the Canadian model—implemented through law rather than policy—is indeed viewed as an excessive deterrent to attracting researchers, then it should not be pursued. On the other hand, if the Qatar Foundation and QNRF perceive that protecting the rights that concern the national interest are paramount, then opting for a statute-based version of the Canadian model might be most prudent. In addition to these considerations, the choice of model should be informed by a comparative assessment of the transaction costs and administrative burden of the two models.

The fund ownership model and the joint ownership model, however, are not assignment schema that we would advise QNRF to pursue. While each vests considerable more apparent power in the hands of QNRF, both are far out of step with what foreign researchers have come to expect and are likely to act as a significant deterrent for researchers who have particularly novel or valuable projects that could receive funding elsewhere. Given the fund's dependence on foreign research talent (particularly during its initial years), QNRF should be wary about staking out such a position. Indeed, even if QNRF stood willing to negotiate private arrangements with each recipient on a case-by-case basis, such a practice is costly and time-consuming and ultimately probably not worth the time and effort if an alternative default allocation better fits the bill. To more completely frame the issue, Table B.2 analyzes the relative strengths and weaknesses of each of the aforementioned approaches.

Concluding Notes

We close with a few small but important notes, the first of which concerns the distinction between university and nonuniversity recipients. Because QNRF will likely be providing research funding to both university researchers and to private firms, it is important that it adopt a clear policy about whether it will distinguish between the two types of recipient insofar as IPR ownership is concerned. While some countries do make such distinctions, the norm is to treat university and nonuniversity researchers similarly.[5] Given an increasing trend toward university-corporate partnerships, the conflicts inherent in an IPR structure in which multiple

---

[5]   Most countries that treat them differently (e.g., Japan) accord greater rights to nonuniversity recipients, apparently under the theory that they have greater entrepreneurial incentives.

Table B.2
Comparisons of Models

Model	Description	Benefits	Costs
Fund ownership	QNRF retains all IPRs and rights to license to third parties. Grantee retains zero royalty (nontransferable) license. Grantee and QNRF may reach alternative allocation on individual basis.	The model gives Qatari control of research output. QNRF receives licensing revenue. The model is highly predictable.	The model is dissimilar to most prevailing models. The model is unlikely to attract foreign researchers in competitive market.
Joint ownership	Grantee and QNRF each assume 50% undivided interest in IPRs. Grantee and QNRF each retain zero royalty license. Grantee and QNRF jointly license to third parties; revenues are divided pro-rata. Grantee and QNRF may reach alternative allocation on a case-by-case basis.	The model gives some Qatari control of research output. The model educes revenue streams from licensing.	The model is dissimilar to most prevailing models. The model is unlikely to attract foreign researchers. The model forces cumbersome negotiations. The model is unpredictable.
Prevailing international	By legal *presumption*, grantee retains IPRs and rights to license. QNRF retains zero royalty license. QNRF retains IPRs in certain exceptional cases; QNRF may also exercise march-in rights when grantee fails to disclose discoveries or fails to exploit IPRs in manner consistent with QNRF goals. Grantee may appeal declaration of exception or exercise of march-in rights, administratively and judicially. QNRF must demonstrate basis for its decision. Grantee and QNRF may reach alternative allocation on individual basis.	The model is identical to most prevailing models. The model provides incentives to do research in Qatar. The model is likely to attract foreign researchers. The model encourages exploitation of revenues in Qatar.	The model is administratively cumbersome. The model is less flexible than it first appears. The model reduces Qatari control over research output. The model produces little direct licensing revenue for Qatar.
Canadian	QNRF formally retains IPRs but, in most cases, adopts a formal policy that favors assignment to grantee. QNRF retains zero royalty license. QNRF retains IPRs in certain cases; QNRF may also exercise march-in rights when grantee fails to disclose discoveries or fails to exploit IPRs in manner consistent with QNRF goals. Grantee may appeal QNRF's declaration of exception or exercise of march-in rights. Grantee must demonstrate that QNRF's actions were arbitrary, capricious, or abuse of discretion. Grantee and QNRF may reach alternative allocation on a case-by-case basis.	This is similar to most prevailing models. It provides incentives to do research in Qatar. It is likely to attract foreign researchers. It encourages exploitation of revenues in Qatar. It gives some administrative flexibility.	It reduces Qatari control over research output (but gives more than under BDA model). It provides little direct licensing revenue for Qatar. It modestly reduces predictability (relative to BDA model).

recipients exist, and the challenge of crafting a parsimonious IPR policy, we see good reasons to treat university and private recipients in substantially similar (if not identical) fashions.

Second, in many cases, institutions and their constituent researchers may have their own agreements about who receives title to IPRs produced during the course of research. In most modern contexts, the institution retains the rights, but it is not difficult to find instances in which an individual researcher negotiates for an enhanced entitlement. We see little reason for QNRF to attempt to intercede into these arrangements. Rather, regardless of the package of IPRs that the grantee ultimately receives, this package should be freely assignable between the institution and researcher (subject, however, to any disclosure and exploitation requirements, which would apply to either party).

Third, as noted, the underlying IPR allocation regime in most states is considered a *default* regime and is subject to revision through negotiation between the funding entity and the recipient. We envision that QNRF would similarly allow for such negotiated tailoring in some cases (keeping in mind, of course, the transaction costs implicit in such endeavors). Indeed, the four models explored above all provide for an individual grantee and QNRF to negotiate alternative IPR allocations in appropriate circumstances. One way in which such tailoring might take place is through designation of specific grant types by QNRF. For instance, if QNRF adopted a general policy that largely tracked the BDA (and thus gave recipients presumptive ownership of IPRs), it could still designate certain projects as contract work, in which the recipient must assign rights to QNRF as a funding condition. Such designations would be appropriate when, for example, the output of the research is likely to be a pioneering technology that is capable of generating substantial follow-on innovations. Facilitating access to that pioneering technology for improvers may catalyze the creation of valuable and marketable applications. Such designations, in conjunction with a default entitlement regime, are likely to give QNRF even greater flexibility in defining both its portfolio of research projects and its ultimate ownership rights.

Fourth, as previously noted, regardless of who receives the ultimate assignment of IPRs, it is relatively common for the nonrecipient to receive a nonexclusive, nontransferable right to use IP for its own purposes. Such a reservation of rights seems sensible in this context as well. For example, under either the Canadian model or the prevailing international model, QNRF would maintain a right to use the content of the invention in its own activities or to provide essential research tools for later funded projects. The nonrecipient would not, however, be free to sell licenses to third parties as a source of revenue.

Finally, it is important to remain aware of the parameters of Qatari law regarding IP. Qatar is a signatory to the principal international accords on IPR protection; however, the internal laws of Qatar are still not well developed in the areas of copyright and patents. While we presume that most foreign researchers would likely attempt to procure foreign patent rights for subject inventions, there may be some contexts in which either a grantee or QNRF will attempt to perfect IPRs within Qatar. A local expert in these areas may prove to be an exceptionally useful asset for consultations on what constraints (if any) such local patenting would place on QNRF's adopted approach.[6]

---

[6] For example, some of our interviews with members of the Qatari IP community revealed that contractual agreements allocating IPRs between an individual researcher and his or her institution may not be accorded complete protection under the patent code in the Cooperation Council for the Arab States of the Gulf (GCC). Others disagreed with this assessment. This disagreement may reflect a current state of flux in domestic law regarding patents—a topic that a local expert would be in a good position to analyze.

References

Alfred P. Sloan Foundation, "How to Apply for a Grant," undated Web page (a). As of August 6, 2007:
http://www.sloan.org/grant/index.shtml

———, "Programs: Standard of Living and Economic Performance: Industry Studies," undated Web page (b). As of August 23, 2007:
http://www.sloan.org/programs/IndustryStudies.shtml

———, "2006 Annual Report: Science and Technology: Sloan Research Fellowships," 2006. As of August 23, 2007:
http://www.sloan.org/report/2006/research_fellowships.shtml

Aspen Institute, *Foundation Accountability and Effectiveness, A Statement for Public Discussion*, Washington, D.C.: Nonprofit Sector Strategy Group, the Aspen Institute, 2002. As of August 6, 2007:
http://www.aspeninstitute.org/atf/cf/{DEB6F227-659B-4EC8-8F84-8DF23CA704F5}/PHILANTHROPY.PDF

BES—*see* U.S. Department of Energy, Office of Basic Energy Sciences.

Bill and Melinda Gates Foundation, "About Us: Quick Facts," undated Web page (a). As of August 23, 2007:
http://www.gatesfoundation.org/AboutUs/QuickFacts/default.htm

———, "Foundation Facts," undated Web page (b). As of August 6, 2007:
http://www.gatesfoundation.org/MediaCenter/FactSheet/

Boston Foundation, *Assessing Foundation Performance: Current Practices, Future Possibilities*, Boston, Mass.: Center for Effective Philanthropy, November 14–15, 2002. As of August 6, 2007:
http://www.effectivephilanthropy.org/images/pdfs/cep02seminar.pdf

Buchanan, Phil, *Foundation Governance: The CEO Viewpoint*, Cambridge, Mass.: Center for Effective Philanthropy, February 2004. As of August 6, 2007:
http://www.effectivephilanthropy.org/images/pdfs/governanceceoview.pdf

Carnegie Corporation of New York, "Andrew Carnegie's Vision for Carnegie Corporation," undated Web page. As of August 23, 2007:
http://www.carnegie.org/sub/philanthropy/carn_vis_carn.html

Center for Effective Philanthropy, *Toward a Common Language: Listening to Foundation CEOs and Other Experts Talk About Performance Measurement in Philanthropy*, Boston, Mass.: Center for Effective Philanthropy, February 2002a. As of August 6, 2007:
http://www.effectivephilanthropy.org/images/pdfs/towardacommonlanguage.pdf

———, *Indicators of Effectiveness: Understanding and Improving Foundation Performance: Report on the Foundation Performance Metrics Pilot Study*, Boston, Mass.: Center for Effective Philanthropy, August 2002b. As of August 6, 2007:
http://www.effectivephilanthropy.org/images/pdfs/indicatorsofeffectiveness.pdf

CEP—*see* Center for Effective Philanthropy.

DARPA—*see* Defense Advanced Research Projects Agency.

Defense Advanced Research Projects Agency, "DARPA Mission," last updated March 27, 2007. As of August 6, 2007:
http://www.darpa.mil/body/mission.html

Diamond v. Chakrabarty, 447 U.S. 303, 100 S. Ct. 2204, June 16, 1980.

Economic Review Committee Sub-Committee on Entrepreneurship and Internationalisation, *Recommendations on Government in Business*, May 30, 2002. As of August 6, 2007:
http://app.mti.gov.sg/data/pages/507/doc/ERC_EISC_MainReport.pdf

EISC—*see* Economic Review Committee Sub-Committee on Entrepreneurship and Internationalisation.

Foundation for Research, Science, and Technology, "About Us," undated Web page. As of August 6, 2007:
http://www.frst.govt.nz/About/

———, *Annual Report for the Year Ended 30 June 2003*, Wellington, N.Z., October 2003a.

———, *Statement of Intent, 2003–2006: Investing in Innovation for New Zealand's Future*, Wellington, N.Z., October 2003b.

FRST—*see* Foundation for Research, Science, and Technology.

Global Leaders for Tomorrow, *Philanthropy Measures Up*, January 28, 2003. As of August 6, 2007:
http://www.effective-philanthropy.org/images/pdfs/philanthropymeasuresup.pdf

GLT—*see* Global Leaders for Tomorrow.

Guidice, Philip Michael, and Kevin Bolduc, *Assessing Performance at the Robert Wood Johnson Foundation: A Case Study*, Cambridge, Mass.: Center for Effective Philanthropy, 2004. As of September 10, 2007:
http://www.effectivephilanthropy.org/images/pdfs/RWJFcasestudy.pdf

Heller, Michael A., and Rebecca S. Eisenberg, "Can Patents Deter Innovation? The Anticommons in Biomedical Research," *Science*, Vol. 280, No. 5364, May 1998, pp. 698–701.

HHS—*see* U.S. Department of Health and Human Services.

KACST—*see* King Abdulaziz City for Science and Technology.

King Abdulaziz City for Science and Technology, "About Us," undated Web page. As of August 6, 2007:
http://www.kacst.edu.sa/eng/aboutus.php

Massachusetts Institute of Technology, Undergraduate Research Opportunities Program, "Basic Information," undated Web page. As of August 23, 2007:
http://web.mit.edu/UROP/basicinfo/index.html

Michael Smith Foundation for Health Research, "Terms of Reference," approved August 23, 2001, last updated December 6, 2001. As of August 6, 2007:
http://www.msfhr.org/sub-about-people-research-terms.htm

———, "About Us," last updated August 17, 2006. As of August 6, 2007:
http://www.msfhr.org/sub-about.htm

Mowery, David C., Richard R. Nelson, Bhaven N. Sampat, and Arvids A. Ziedonis, "The Growth of Patenting and Licensing by U.S. Universities: An Assessment of the Effects of the Bayh-Dole Act of 1980," *Research Policy*, Vol. 30, No. 1, 2001, pp. 99–120.

MSFHR—*see* Michael Smith Foundation for Health Research.

National Institutes of Health, "About NIH," last reviewed July 18, 2007a. As of August 6, 2007:
http://www.nih.gov/about

———, "Office of Extramural Research," last reviewed August 6, 2007b. As of August 6, 2007:
http://grants.nih.gov/grants/oer.htm

National Science Foundation, *Research Experiences for Undergraduates (REU): Supplements and Sites: Program Solicitation*, Washington, D.C., NSF 03-577, undated. As of August 6, 2007:
http://www.nsf.gov/pubs/2003/nsf03577/nsf03577.pdf

———, "National Science Foundation History," last updated March 31, 2006a. As of August 6, 2007:
http://www.nsf.gov/about/history/

———, *Strategic Plan*, September 2006b. As of August 23, 2007:
http://www.nsf.gov/pubs/2006/nsf0648/nsf0648.jsp

———, "Research Experiences for Undergraduates (REU): Sites and Supplements," last updated November 7, 2006c. As of August 23, 2007:
http://www.nsf.gov/pubs/2007/nsf07569/nsf07569.htm

———, "Research Experiences for Undergraduates (REU)," last updated June 22, 2007: As of August 23, 2007:
http://www.nsf.gov/funding/pgm_summ.jsp?pims_id=5517&from=fund

New York State Foundation for Science, Technology, and Innovation, "Goals," undated Web page. As of August 6, 2007:
http://www.nystar.state.ny.us/goals.htm

NIH—*see* National Institutes of Health.

NSF—*see* National Science Foundation.

NYSTAR—*see* New York State Foundation for Science, Technology, and Innovation.

OECD—*see* Organisation for Economic Co-Operation and Development.

Organisation for Economic Co-Operation and Development, *Turning Science into Business: Patenting and Licensing at Public Research Organisations*, Paris, France: Organisation for Economic Co-Operation and Development, 2003.

Public Law 81-507, The National Science Foundation Act of 1950, May 10, 1950.

Public Law 96-480, Stevenson-Wylder Technology Innovation Act of 1980, October 21, 1980.

Public Law 96-517, Patent and Trademark Act Amendments of 1980, December 12, 1980.

Qatar Foundation—*see* Qatar Foundation for Education, Science, and Community Development.

Qatar Foundation for Education, Science, and Community Development, "Our Vision and Mission," last updated May 7, 2007. As of August 6, 2007:
http://www.qf.edu.qa/output/page293.asp

Rai, Arti K., and Rebecca S. Eisenberg, "Bayh-Dole Reform and the Progress of Biomedicine," *Law and Contemporary Problems*, Vol. 66, Nos. 1–2, Winter–Spring 2003, pp. 289–314.

Robert Wood Johnson Foundation, "Our Mission," undated Web page. As of August 6, 2007:
http://www.rwjf.org/about/mission.jhtml

RWJF—*see* Robert Wood Johnson Foundation.

Science Foundation Ireland, *Vision 2004–2008: People, Ideas and Partnerships for a Globally Competitive Irish Research System*, undated. As of August 6, 2007:
http://www.sfi.ie/content/content.asp?section_id=314&language_id=1

SFI—*see* Science Foundation Ireland.

UROP—*see* Massachusetts Institute of Technology.

U.S. Code, Title 35, Section 202, Disposition of Rights.

U.S. Department of Energy, Office of Basic Energy Sciences, *Office of Science Strategic Plan*, February 12, 2004. As of August 23, 2007:
http://www.sc.doe.gov/bes/archives/plans/SCSP_12FEB04.pdf

U.S. Department of Health and Human Services, Public Health Service, *Progress Report for a Public Health Service Grant*, Washington, D.C.: U.S. Department of Health and Human Services, instructions PHS 2590, revised September 2004, interim revision April 2006. As of August 20, 2007:
http://grants.nih.gov/grants/funding/2590/phs2590.pdf